*Masters of Equitation
on Collecting and
Lengthening*

Masters of Equitation on Collecting and Lengthening

Compiled by
Martin Diggle

J. A. Allen
London

© Martin Diggle 2002
First Published in Great Britain 2002

ISBN 0 85131 848 7

J.A. Allen
Clerkenwell House
Clerkenwell Green
London EC1R 0HT

J.A. Allen is an imprint of Robert Hale Ltd

The right of Martin Diggle to be identified as compiler of this work has been
asserted by him in accordance with the Copyright, Designs and Patents Act 1988

British Library Cataloguing in Publication Data
A catalogue record for this book is available from the British Library

All extracts from *Dressage A Study of the Finer Points of Riding* by Henry Wynmalen
are reproduced by permission of the Wilshire Book Company (California, USA);
from *Horsemanship* by Waldemar Seunig by permission of Robert Hale Ltd.; from
Riding Logic by Wilhelm Müseler by permission of The Random House Group
Ltd.; from *The Complete Training of Horse and Rider* by Alois Podhajsky by permission
of The Sportsman's Press; from *The Gymnasium of the Horse* by Gustav Steinbrecht
by permission of Xenophon Press (Cleveland Heights, Ohio, USA).

The following photographs and illustrations are also reproduced by permission:
Collected, medium and extended walk (pages 28–9) (artwork Brian Tutlo), Excelso
in extended trot (page 134) (photo Paul Belasik), A phase of extended trot not
often depicted (page 135) and Paul Belasik riding extended canter (page 150) (pho-
tos Karl Leck) from Belasik's *Dressage for the 21st Century* by permission of those
named; The school gaits (page 109) from Knopfhart's *Dressage A Guidebook for the
Road to Success* by permission of Half Halt Press Inc. (PO Box 67, Boonboro,
Maryland 21756, USA).

Jacket photograph of the compiler by permission of Mike Freeman

The compiler and publisher acknowledge all of these generous permissions with
thanks. Despite our best efforts we have been unable to trace ownership of the
copyright of some material included in this book. If anyone feels that they have a
claim, please contact the publisher.

Design by Nancy Lawrence
Series compiler Martin Diggle
Colour separation by Tenon & Polert Colour Scanning Ltd
Printed in Singapore by Kyodo Printing Co (S'pore) Pte Ltd

Contents

Introduction to the Masters of Equitation on Dressage Series

When we first discover a new pursuit, most of us explore it with more enthusiasm than science. This is necessarily so, since our desire to participate greatly exceeds our understanding of the principles involved. It is when we begin actively to seek a greater understanding of these principles that we can be sure that we have acquired a genuine new interest, and are not simply indulging a passing fad.

In our quest for knowledge, we look first to the nearest and most obvious sources. If our new interest is riding, we acquire an instructor, listen (hopefully) to what we are told, and begin to question the apparent paradoxes of equitation as they unfold. With time, our field of information broadens; we learn what our instructor has been told by his or her instructor, we begin to follow the exploits of top riders in the different disciplines, and we even start to read books.

It is at some point along this path that we start to realise just what a wealth of knowledge we have at our disposal. We also begin to realise that much of this knowledge is far from new. There is initial surprise when we learn that the elderly gentleman who trains our current idol was, himself, an Olympic medallist – a further surprise that he, in turn, was trained by a cavalry officer famed, in his time, as a leading light of the Cadre Noir. We discover in a book written forty or fifty years ago ideas of which we were unaware, and then marvel at the extensive references to writers long dead before the author's own birth. We regard, with awe, faded, grainy photographs of riders whose positions – even to our untutored eyes – look positively centaur-like, and we are bemused by ancient diagrams of school movements that make today's dressage tests seem like a hack in the park.

If, at this point, we pause to reflect a little, we start to see this heritage in its true context. It is a common human conceit to believe that we, or our near contemporaries, are the first to discover anything, but this is very rarely true. So far as riding is concerned, it is no exaggeration to say that it is, in absolute terms, less important to us than it was to our ancestors. If we need to prove this point we can consider that, three hundred years ago, a poorly ridden lateral movement might result in decapitation by an enemy sabre. The same movement, ridden today, would result in an 'insufficient' on the test sheet, and a wounded ego.

Of course, not all equitation historically was concerned with the vital necessities of war. Certainly since the Renaissance, there have always been people fascinated by the *art* of riding – interestingly, this group includes a number of Masters who were, first and foremost, military men.

It is in the nature of art to give birth to experimentation, innovation and re-interpretation, and it is in the nature of artists to be influenced by – even to borrow from – others, and yet still develop their own styles. Sometimes, in pursuit of new ideas, an acknowledged Master may stray too far down a particular path, causing even his most admiring pupils to question the wisdom of the route, but such instances have a way of triggering the reassessment and consolidation of major principles.

All of these things have happened in equitation, against a

background of different types and breeds of horses, and varying equestrian requirements. Not surprisingly, this has given rise to a number of schools, or philosophies, which place different degrees of emphasis on certain principles. By delving into the wealth of literature available, it is possible for the avid reader to discover these philosophies, and draw from them ideas and information which may be of personal value. However, because of the volume of material available, and the need to embark upon a major voyage of discovery, this can be considered an extensive – albeit rewarding – process.

The purpose behind the *Masters of Equitation* series is to gather together, under individual subject headings, many of the key thoughts of eminent equestrians, thus providing a convenient source of reference to their ideas. The reader is invited to research, compare and contrast – and may find a special significance in areas of obvious consensus.

Compiler's Note

In producing this series of books, the aims of the publisher are twofold. First, it is certainly the intention that they should act as reference works, giving readers with specific schooling queries access to the thoughts of many Masters in a single volume.

Second, it is very much hoped that they will act as an appetiser, a stimulus for further reading of the original works cited and, indeed, for Classical equestrian works in general.

With regard to this latter aim, I can foresee that some readers, who have already made a study of the Classics, may search this book in vain for their favourite extract or author. If this happens, I beg such readers' pardon. The truth is, in order to be completely comprehensive, a book such as this would have to quote great swathes of material from very many sources – an undertaking that would exhaust the energies of compiler, publisher and perhaps even the most ardent reader!

Further to this, it has been stated that the whole aim of the older School of Classical equitation was to set the horse on his haunches. In other words, the minds of the older Classical Masters were greatly exercised by the aim, not only of obtaining collection, but of obtaining the ultimate degree of collection, which would prepare their horses to perform the High School airs. (Constraint of space does not allow the inclusion of material on these airs, but any reader who questions the roles that power and energy play in true collection may find these older works salutary reading.) While the overall emphasis upon this degree of collection has moderated down the years, it remains the case that Classical authorities view collection, and the work towards it, as a keystone of equitation. As a consequence, very large parts of the older Classical books, and considerable sections of more recent ones, deal either directly with collection, or indirectly with related topics. Patently, such a volume of material cannot be reproduced here. However, I am mindful of the relevance of these related topics, since they highlight the point that, important though collection is, the Masters are at pains to discuss it in context, rather than in isolation. In the more recent works, as lengthening the stride takes on greater importance, this, too, is seen in context – not least, of course, with collection. Therefore, while most of the extracts reproduced here deal overtly with collecting and lengthening, I have tried to include a few which indicate the relationship between these and other aspects of training, in the hope that they may encourage the reader to explore these inter-relationships more fully in the original works.

Finally, I would point out that this book does not include material on those ultimately collected forms of trot – passage and piaffe – since the intention is that they will be subjects for another title in this series.

Introduction to the Masters of Equitation on Collecting and Lengthening

It is hardly overstating the case to say that, historically, collection was the primary aim of training, and yet it remains one of the most widely misunderstood aspects of equitation. Because of the key role it plays, misconceptions about collection will impede not only the correct development of 'collected' work, but also the progression of the overall training programme. Lengthening the gaits, which has assumed an increasing importance in modern times with the development of the sport horse, is similarly subject to much misinterpretation.

Yet, performed correctly, collection and extension will act harmoniously to develop longitudinal suppleness, balance and power – qualities which are highly desirable both inside and outside the dressage arena.

Through the words of the Masters, this book endeavours to provide valuable insights to the real aims and correct introduction of these gait variants, and it is hoped that the guidance given will be of assistance to all who wish to advance their horses' training correctly and progressively.

In accord with earlier books in this series, I would reiterate the point that many European writers have traditionally used the French *galop* (which serves for both canter and gallop) when referring to the three-beat gait of canter. With particular reference to the subject matter of this book, I would also point out that the definitions of the gait variants in current use (collected, working, medium, extended) have, to some extent, evolved down the years. Some writers of earlier generations used different terms from these – in some cases, to describe slightly different forms of the gaits.[1] However, where such uses appear in the following pages, the *type* of gait variant referred to will be evident from the context.

Other terms with which some readers may be unfamiliar are the French *ramener* and *rassembler*. One might say that the former relates primarily to head carriage – the closing of the angle of the head with the neck, via flexion at the poll, which remains the highest point – while the latter describes an overall state of collection. However, as will become clear, these basic definitions are subject to refinement and expansion by the Masters, and the explanations they offer provide extra insight to the underlying subject of collection.

---

[1] Readers interested in this topic might be fascinated by the chapter The Working Trot in Dr H.L.M. van Schaik's *Misconceptions and Simple Truths in Dressage.*

The Historical Development of Collecting and Lengthening

Why, in equitation, is there an emphasis on collecting and lengthening the stride? What is the purpose of doing so, and what are the benefits?

In order to gain an understanding of any subject, it is always instructive to consider its historical development. Those involved in this development have almost certainly asked – and answered – many of the 'how?' and 'why?' questions that may occur to us. Such thinkers and innovators will also have incorporated new ideas, discoveries and demands into their theories and practice. In simple terms, they have done much of our thinking for us. As we study equitation, it is further to our advantage that the acknowledged Masters are, themselves, among the most assiduous students: we therefore have the benefit of being able to study developments through their expert, analytical eyes.

It is interesting to note that some of the purposes and benefits of adjusting the stride had been discovered as long ago as the fourth century BC:

He must be collected at the turns, because it is not easy or safe for the horse to make short turns when he is at full speed, especially if the ground is uneven or slippery. When the rider collects him, he must not throw the horse aslant at all with the bit, nor sit at all aslant himself...The moment the horse faces the stretch after finishing the turn, the rider should push him on to go faster.   Xenophon *The Art of Horsemanship*

Xenophon was clearly aware of the role that collection can play in enhancing balance, and presumably some form of lengthening was involved in 'going on faster'.

   Leaping over 2000 years ahead, we see the French Master, de la Guérinière, giving reasons for variations of gait:

M. de la Broue [Salomon de la Broue] says that a proper gallop should be short in the forehand and energetic in the hind-quarters. The definition applies to the School gallop, of which we speak here; for the gallop of hunting horses, of which we shall speak in the chapter devoted to that subject, should be extended.

Although this extension should not be to the point at which balance is lost:

When beginning to gallop a horse destined for the hunt, the gait should not at first be too extended, because not being used to galloping freely, the horse will lean on the hand. Neither should the gallop be too collected, which would inhibit movement. The horse should gallop naturally, without being held back or pushed on too much, as if it were galloping by itself, without a rider. A light hand, together with frequent *descentes de main* produces such a gallop.
                    François Robichon de la Guérinière *School of Horsemanship*

It is evident that de la Guérinière is making a clear distinction between the demands of High School work and the practicalities of cross-country riding. In this, as in so many respects, he was a man in advance of his time – the comment on galloping 'naturally' seems to presage the ideas of Caprilli[1] by a century and a half.

De la Guérinière also comments on the use of varying the gait in the preparation of individual horses for school work:

The nature of each horse must be carefully assessed, in order to tailor its training thereto. Horses which withhold their strength should be made to go at an extended gait on long, straight lines before regulating their gallop; those too spirited should, on the contrary, be kept in a slow, short gallop, which prevents them from hurrying...

François Robichon de la Guérinière *School of Horsemanship*

De la Guérinière's 'extension' should, however, be seen as relative to a considerable degree of collection – he writes elsewhere of 'the extended, brisk trot' on a circle, which is clearly not the extended trot as ridden nowadays. Also, while it is true that he understood the practicalities of riding beyond the confines of the school, it is also the case that his school work – albeit enlightened and innovative – continued substantially in the High School traditions. The crux of this High School work had been summarised earlier by The Duke of Newcastle:

A horse that does not go well upon his haunches, can never do well in the Manege [sic], so that our whole study is to put him upon them...

William Cavendish, Duke of Newcastle *A General System of Horsemanship*

---

[1] Federico Caprilli, active and influential at the turn of the nineteenth century, advocated (in the words of W.S. Felton) 'that for cross-country riding no effort should be made to require the horse to change his natural carriage, leaving it to the horse to make such modifications in his natural balance as conditions might require...'

This can be seen as pretty unequivocal emphasis upon collecting the school horse. It is noteworthy, however, that Newcastle goes on to emphasise the need for *correct* collection:

I would have you understand, when a horse may properly be said to be upon his haunches, and when not. Suppose a horse to be almost sitting upon his croupe, he is not upon his haunches notwithstanding, if his hind-legs are distant from the lines of nature (which is to have them much asunder,) although he is almost upon his croupe. But to be upon his haunches, his hind-legs ought to be in their natural position, with the haunch-bone pointing directly forward, and his hind-legs under his belly, bending his hocks as much as possible; and this is the just situation of a horse upon his haunches.

William Cavendish, Duke of Newcastle *A General System of Horsemanship*

(Newcastle also makes the point that horses unsuited to highly collected work may have valuable roles in other fields.)

It is evident, therefore, that (certainly in the school and substantially outside it) an almost total emphasis upon collection continued after the Renaissance period, through the eighteenth century and, indeed, beyond. This situation is summed up by Paul Belasik:

In Pignatelli's time (the sixteenth century), in the Duke of Newcastle's and Pluvinel's times (the seventeenth century), and then later in Guérinière's era (the eighteenth century), the whole object of dressage was to get the horse upon the haunches. To a great extent, the clear goals of jumping the horse off its hind legs (the high school airs), tested many a trainer's idea of collection. There was no question about where the balance was or, better still, where it should be. A trainer might fail, but he would know what he was trying to achieve...

Being able to change the balance of the horse and redistribute weight off the forehand could save these weaker limbs in transitions, thus offering them physical relief and freedom of expression.

Paul Belasik *Dressage for the 21st Century*

Belasik's passage, which introduces a discussion of equine balance, also points to the reasons *why* there was such an emphasis on collection. The primary reason can be seen, essentially, to be tradition. While there are differing views about the extent to which the High School airs were associated with battle manoeuvres, it is undoubtedly true that they were seen, for several centuries, as epitomising the artistic element of equitation, and this was considered highly important. The second reason was that true collection greatly enhances balance and control – qualities of unquestionable value – and the supplementary reason was that rebalancing the horse through collection reduced the incidence of foreleg injury and increased his longevity.

It is, no doubt, true that all the genuine Masters retained a respect for the equestrian artistry of their predecessors. During the nineteenth century, Gustav Steinbrecht wrote:

The old masters knew how to thoroughly work the haunches and have become a lasting example for us for years to come. Their extraordinary accomplishments, which at present are considered to be almost miracles, were the result of only this work. If we are serious in maintaining the equestrian art as a fine art and not let it be degraded to philistinism and puppetry, there is only one way: we must follow the old masters.

Gustav Steinbrecht *The Gymnasium of the Horse*

However, Steinbrecht was equally appreciative of the practicalities linked to the art...

To make the hind legs flexible and able to carry weight is the main purpose of dressage training, partially because it gives the rider an opportunity to correctly relieve the forelegs...Only in this way is it possible to keep the horse sound, fresh, and surefooted as well as suitable for service under the rider up to a high age.

...an appreciation that was heightened by his veterinary studies:

By nature, the forelegs are intended primarily as supports for the body; due to their structure, they are capable of moving forward uniformly with the hind legs to support the forward-driven body mass at the proper time; but they do not possess any thrust or spring force to move the body forward independently...The bones of the hindquarters, however, are arranged at angles to one another and, with their spring-action joints, are capable of pushing the body mass forward with greater force or, if the mass acts in a more perpendicular direction, of thrusting it upward...The hindquarters are thus the main seat of all displays of power by the horse...   Gustav Steinbrecht *The Gymnasium of the Horse*

These practical points have been echoed down the years:

A horse on its haunches is one which lowers and brings them under the body, while putting the hind feet forward under the belly, in order to give itself a natural balance in counterbalance to the forehand, which is the weaker part. It is from this balance that the quality and lightness of the mouth come.
        François Robichon de la Guérinière *School of Horsemanship*

Most horses...will carry a greater proportion of their weight on the forehand, a fact which will be still more noticeable when the rider mounts. The hind legs will push the weight more than they carry it, a fault which must be corrected if the paces are to be made as light and elastic as is expected from a school horse.

The object of training will be to correct the balance by making the hindquarters carry a greater proportion of the weight and to relieve the forehand by transferring the weight from the shoulders to the quarters...

Collection is necessary for advanced training as it makes the hindquarters carry a greater proportion of the weight and thus relieves the forehand. In this way it will also prevent the horse from wearing out his forelegs prematurely...collection increases balance (thus improving contact), develops the paces, and establishes obedience.

Alois Podhajsky *The Complete Training of Horse and Rider*

When it has to carry the weight of the rider, an untrained horse will overload its forelegs and will very soon damage them if it is not educated to redistribute the weight more equally over all four limbs... Alfred Knopfhart *Fundamentals of Dressage*

With all these artistic and practical reasons for its pursuit, it is hardly surprising that the emphasis remained heavily upon collection – not only in the school but, to a significant extent, across country – for a considerable time. Commenting on the attempts of the nineteenth-century French Commandant, the Comte d'Aure, to adapt school riding to the demands of the cavalry, W.S. Felton wrote:

Lest we overemphasize the extent of the change as it had developed in the lifetime of the Comte d'Aure we must not forget that all of the riders of the classical school used a high degree of collection so that, even as modified for cross-country, the accepted technique still required a degree of collection which would not today be considered desirable.

W.S. Felton *Masters of Equitation*

At the same time that riders such as d'Aure were beginning to adapt Classical methods to the demands of cross-country riding, the controversial François Baucher, whose sole interest was in school riding, appeared on the scene. Here, Felton makes a comparison between Baucher's practices and those of his erstwhile disciple, James Fillis, citing equine development as one of the factors in Fillis's relative progression towards more forward movement:

Even in the brief period which elapsed between Baucher and Fillis, horses of better breeding had become available. So whereas Baucher's horses, though better bred than many previously used for school riding, were still relatively thick and heavy necked, we find Fillis using much finer horses...Perhaps it was partly because of the better horses he was training that we find him constantly emphasizing the importance of forward motion, but what he was seeking was not at all the free forward movement of the cross-country horse nor the extended gaits required of the present-day dressage rider, but rather the controlled impulse of the horse constantly moving in collection.

W.S. Felton *Masters of Equitation*

It seems, therefore, that two factors influencing the broader development of equitation were an increasing demand for cross-country riding (in forms in which the horse was something more than a mere beast of burden), and developments in the actual types of horses available. Felton summarises these factors thus:

With the faster pace of the twentieth century, interest in the faster moving cross-country horse was to supersede to a considerable extent interest in the slower collected movements of the school rider. The stage was set for a revolution.

W.S. Felton *Masters of Equitation*

Dr H.L.M. van Schaik and his great admirer, Paul Belasik, also discuss the gradual changes that took place throughout the nineteenth century:

After the French Revolution, there developed in Europe an interest in the English Thoroughbred and the way the English rode in the field. As a result, we find in the literature the beginning of the description of the strong trot (French 'grand trot', German 'starker Trab'). For example Hünersdorf (1800) writes about the lengthening of the stride…He claims that the advantage of this movement is that the horse learns how to lengthen himself, is strengthened by these exercises, and is taught to go forward with head and neck correctly placed.

The Comte d'Aure (1852) wrote that speed is not obtained by allowing the horse to go forward in an impetuous way. The fact that d'Aure asks a group of riders to execute the lengthened trot…on a circle proves that the length of this trot was far less than the length of the modern extended trot. Nowadays, the extended trot is not being asked on the circle, because it is impossible. Rather, it is the medium trot that now is asked on the circle.

Faverot de Kerbrech (1891), interpreter of Baucher, writes that the strong trot ('grand trot') should be progressively developed out of the ordinary trot ('petit trot'). The movement should be free and resolute; the head should be close to the perpendicular, and the horse should go energetically and straight forward.

When reading these quotations, one has to remember that the authors lived in an era when the basics of equitation were still the engaging of the hindquarters and gymnasticising of the back.

Dr H.L.M. van Schaik *Misconceptions and Simple Truths in Dressage*

Pluvinel, Guérinière, and the riders throughout the Golden Age of Versailles (and sources back toward Xenophon) all hailed and promoted the 'Spanish' (Iberian) type of horse as the best in the world for dressage. Trainers universally sought a horse of average size, close-coupled, with quick reflexes, but good dispositions. They looked for 'uphill' horses that were naturally built for collection. In the late nineteenth and early twentieth centuries this changed. Constantly rearming, armies had collected large supplies of crossbred horses. Breeders across Europe were developing a horse in a 'rectangular' frame. This was a horse that at first was heavily infused with Thoroughbred blood; one that could be multidisciplinary. It was a horse first for cavalry use, and then a horse that could run, jump and hunt as well as perform in dressage competitions...

It was the cavalry officers – now facing the mechanization of the armies – who began in the late nineteenth century, and then more formally in the early twentieth century, to compete against each other at dressage shows, among other disciplines. Quite naturally, the officers competed on their own horses. These new horses were generally larger than the old Spanish type, and often proportionally longer backed. As more carriage-type horses were used in breeding, the 'new' horse continued to develop a long suspended trot, which quite simply became the fashion of the entire century in the competition arena...

There was also an increasing infatuation with sports of the field. The Italian Federico Caprilli's elegant jumping style was seen as revolutionary, being practically the diametric opposite of the school riding that had started in his own country a few hundred years earlier...

In terms of competition dressage, the shift to the new 'rectangular' type of horse was very nearly universal. The FEI was essentially giving tacit approval through the markings of its judges, which were biased toward the new kind of horse. Read Podhajsky's accounts of trying to compete with his Lipizzaners and the response to them as opposed to the Thoroughbred types he had been so successful with. This kind of endorsement by the international body went a long way toward standardizing the type of horse that would be successful at their competitions.

Further on in his analysis, Belasik brings us up to date in respect of the development of collecting and lengthening:

In terms of performance, the twentieth century rounded out the practice of dressage by placing more equal emphasis on all gaits, and collection *and* extension within every gait.

Paul Belasik *Dressage for the 21st Century*

The Relationship between Collecting and Lengthening

One misconception is all too common...There are people who have never seen a properly trained manège horse. They have, however, seen falsely trained 'dressage horses', broken down and robbed of their gait and impulsion, and believe that manège training stifles forward impulsion and the capacity for long-striding working gaits. Precisely the contrary is true. In intensified collection...the muscles of the croup, which make the principal contribution to the bending of the haunches...perform the greatest amount of work and are under extraordinary tension when the hindquarters are lowered. This exercise strengthens these muscles...which are equally important as flexors and extensors, to such a degree that the gait of a well-trained manège horse is more energetic, vigorous and elastic in the extended gaits...than a general utility horse.

Waldemar Seunig *Horsemanship*

It is all too easy, on a superficial level, to think of collecting and lengthening simply as 'opposites', but this is to misunderstand the special relationship between them. On a fundamental level, correct collected strides, or correct extended strides, result from allowing the horse to deploy essentially the same amount of energy in different ways. In that sense, rather than being opposites, collection and extension are more like non-identical twins. To continue this analogy, there are several senses in which collection is the 'first-born'. We have already seen, from a look at their historical development, that this is chronologically true. It is also the case in the individual horse, insofar as the horse needs to develop strength and the ability to 'compress' his energy through collected work before he can truly extend. However, putting aside this matter of precedence, there is ample evidence that both forms of movement have come to be seen as essential evidence of the horse's continued development.

The genesis of modern thinking on the relationship between collecting and lengthening is described by Felton in his summary of French equitation at the end of the nineteenth century:

What had not been learned and what it remained for our modern dressage riders to develop was the use of the extended move-ments which, alternated with collection, are such an important part of present day dressage schooling.

W.S. Felton *Masters of Equitation*

Belasik brings the same thought up to the present day...

Unlike the practice of the previous centuries, the modern notion of dressage could not conceivably involve only collection. Today, the horse must be able to collect and extend with equal facility, to the point where, under the most knowledgeable eyes, the transitions within the gait are a more important test of training than the gait itself.

...and crystallises the relationship:

Extensions are, in a sense, relief from collection but they are also proofs of collection. If a horse cannot immediately lengthen the trot, there is a good chance that the previously collected trot had no power. If nothing can be let out, nothing was being stored up. Collection and extension should be like the proverbial cannon – the same amount of gunpowder, only a different angle of the barrel.   Paul Belasik *Dressage for the 21st Century*

Collected (above), medium and extended walk (opposite), showing changing angulation of the haunches, from Paul Belasik's Dressage for the 21st Century.

This relationship is mentioned, in the context of walk, by Alfred Knopfhart:

At the more advanced levels of education a properly extended walk is a sure sign of self-carriage in collection. A horse that has to be held up by the reins in the collected gaits will not extend itself properly when allowed to...it does not relax its back muscles, consequently its steps lack scope and it may even be irregular. It is, therefore, the extended walk that reveals most clearly the quality of the collected walk.

Alfred Knopfhart *Fundamentals of Dressage*

While other authorities point to the 'twin-like' nature of collection and extension...

When one combines impulsion with the flexibility of joints and muscles, as well as elasticity and springiness, extension of gaits are obtained as easily as are their shortening or their elevation. The rider has the ability to play, in a sense, with the forces of the horse whose inflexions and bends are put at his disposal.

Alexis-François L'Hotte *Questions Équestres* (in *Alexis-François L'Hotte The Quest For Lightness in Equitation,* by Hilda Nelson)

The trainer must devote his undivided attention to working the hind legs...if he wants to bring out of his horse everything that nature has put into it. He has accomplished this, and trained the horse to perfection, if he has brought the two forces...*thrust and carrying power*...to their greatest development.

Gustav Steinbrecht *The Gymnasium of the Horse*

...the influence of the 'first-born' twin...

...it is...certain that the capacity to cadence acquired in the shorter gait, based as it is on increased power and elasticity in the hocks, is an important element in the full development of extension. I will go so far as to say that one cannot succeed fully without it.

Henry Wynmalen *Dressage A Study of the Finer Points of Riding*

...and how the relationship is orchestrated by the rider:

In the collected paces, we strive for cadence, tending towards a moment of suspension; consequently we concentrate more on the lifting effect of the hindlegs than on the driving one...In the extended paces...we concentrate on the driving effect of the hindlegs more than on the lifting one.

Henry Wynmalen *Dressage A Study of the Finer Points of Riding*

These ideas of 'playing' with the horse's forces, and emphasising either the lifting or driving effects are revisited by Belasik, as he reprises his cannon analogy...

Any collection or extension will require a symphonic adjustment of all four legs...This individual suspension will be created by the individual flexion and extension of each leg, and the trajectory of this suspension will be controlled by the aids of the rider. If the tempo remains the same, in collected or extended gaits, the power might be nearly the same. A cannon, if you will, is loaded with a constant amount of gunpowder. The trajectory of the cannon ball, and the overall distance from the cannon at which it comes to earth, are determined by the slant of the cannon barrel. With the cannon pointed up, the trajectory is higher, but that overall distance is shorter. Lower the barrel and the trajectory is lower but longer. In a similar way, the rider controls the trajectory of each of the horse's feet through complex aids, including the bridle.   Paul Belasik *Dressage for the 21st Century*

31

Mrs V.D.S. Williams riding collected trot (above) and extended trot (opposite), from Geoffrey Brooke's Horsemanship, Dressage and Show-Jumping.

...while John Winnett discusses the actions of the horse's limbs, and their relative elevation or extension, in biomechanical terms:

When the horse flexes his neck and poll, this increases the tension of the nuchal and supraspinous ligaments, which brings about the lifting of the thorax, shifting of balance to the rear, rounding of the back, tilting of the lumbosacral joint and the engagement of the hindquarters to the line of maximum lift (this is a perpendicular line through the point of the horse's hip to the

ground). When the hindquarters engage to this line, the articulations of the three joints of the hind leg are coiled for maximum lift off the ground as in collection. On the other hand, when the neck is stretched out and lowered, and the muscles are relaxed and lengthened, the thorax then descends in its sling, shifts balance forward, and allows the hind legs to engage to the line of maximum thrust. (This is a perpendicular line through the horse's centre to the ground. This point can be established by measuring a line from the point of the horse's hip to the point of his shoulder and dividing it in half.) When the hind legs engage to this line, the horse can exert maximum thrust and propulsion from the rear as in extension. Very rarely can a horse

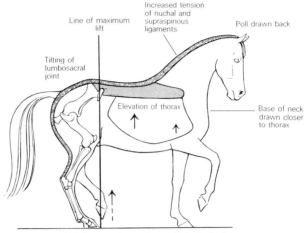

i) Influences for maximum lift (collection)

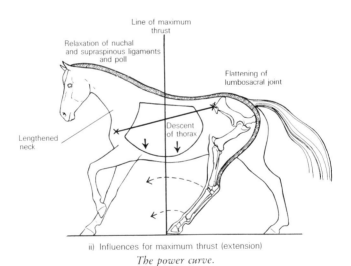

ii) Influences for maximum thrust (extension)

The power curve.

Influences for maximum lift and thrust, from John Winnett's
Dressage as Art in Competition.

engage his hind legs beyond this line, because of the limiting action of the accessory ligament. The more the hind legs engage beyond the line of maximum lift, the more the horse's stride flattens and extends.   John Winnett *Dressage as Art in Competition*

In a reference to the trot, Winnett also makes a point that is crucial to understanding how the same amount of energy is deployed to different effect when collecting or extending...

The rhythm of the trot remains the same whether the trot is collected or extended; only the length of the stride changes.
John Winnett *Dressage as Art in Competition*

...a point that is echoed by Podhajsky:

The difference between the various tempos [i.e. **speeds**] – the ordinary trot, the collected trot, the extended trot – does not lie in the acceleration or the reduction of the pace, but exclusively in the lengthening of the stride or the elevation of the steps while maintaining the rhythm.
Alois Podhajsky *The Complete Training of Horse and Rider*

Others Masters discuss the subtle role of the aids in determining the collection or lengthening of the strides:

Whether flexion or extension predominates at any instant will depend upon the degree of collection. Bracing the seat or opening and closing the fingers must suffice to make thrust predominate over carrying capacity, and vice versa, letting the horse fit into the changed framework with perfect poise.
Waldemar Seunig *Horsemanship*

In concentrating on the influences of the rider's seat, Üdo Burger adds a warning about 'driving' too soon in a horse's education, and in an unconstrained fashion:

We can choose between a passive use of our weight, when we keep our own centre of gravity as close as possible to that of the horse, to form with him a sort of centaur; or, an *active* use of our own weight to displace the horse's centre of gravity...

For example, if we push our seat slightly backward, behind the normal common centre of gravity, an attentive, schooled horse will, of his own accord, tend to flex more the joints of the hindquarters, lighten himself in front and automatically adjust his equilibrium to balance the load. This manner of collection is only possible to a rider who has an upright, relaxed, firm posture and a deep 'vertical' seat. But, if instead of remaining in the 'vertical' seat, the rider drives his buttocks forward (while keeping the upper body upright), he will push the centre of gravity forward and the horse will lengthen his stride...unless his muscles are insufficiently developed, when this pushing effect will only cause him to hurry...

We can use these displacements of weight to shorten or lengthen the strides, to speed up or slow down the beat...However, beyond the narrow limits within which it is effective, the so-called driving seat produces the very opposite of the desired result; it nips the horse under the saddle, presses his back down and impairs the movement of the hindlegs.

Üdo Burger *The Way to Perfect Horsemanship*

Perhaps the ultimate comment on the rider's role in metering out the horse's energy is made by the Portuguese Maestro, Nuno Oliveira. In this passage, which is primarily concerned with the trot, Oliveira makes two telling points: first, that the currently accepted definitions of the gaits (collected, working, medium and extended) are far from all-encompassing and second, that 'feel' and rapport are qualities which can take the rider a step further than sheer technical ability alone:

In the gait known as the trot there are at least ten variations.

First, there is the little trot, not necessarily collected, but rather a trot in which the horse is in a certain state of balance, not over exerting himself or using himself very much. This type of trot is used to relax the nerves while yet exercising an excitable horse.

Then there are two types of collected trot; one having a slower cadence as the horse is pushed on to the bit while yet remaining flexible, and the other having a cadence which is slightly less slow, with the horse's leg action becoming more pronounced and sparkling, but in which the horse is pushed less to go on the bit.

In the medium trot there are at least two more varieties than those of the collected trot.

There are three types to be found in the extended trot; the first being the one in which the horse extends his legs with the greatest energy possible without becoming necessarily completely rigid; another in which the horse is more relaxed, more giving of his back…and the third is the case of the extremely collected horse who throws his fore legs ahead while remaining totally on his haunches. This last trot is the result of the passage or piaffer.

Also, there is the skimming type of trot which becomes a vice in many horses, stemming from rigidity.

Finally, there is the working trot which the Germans use a great deal.

All these varieties of trot are obtained, not by the exclusive use of aids, but rather by knowing the right dosage when demanding action from the horse's nerves; or, conversely, the amount of relaxation to the nervous system, which the rider must encourage at certain moments, applying his own actions, judiciously, in reference to the sensations that the horse gives him.   Nuno Oliveira *Reflections on Equestrian Art*

Defining Collection

It is almost certainly the case that the biggest conceptual problems with collection are rooted in too narrow a definition, and confusion of cause and effect. These errors, especially the latter, are countered in detail in the very fabric of much of the Masters' writings. To begin with, however, here are some thought-provoking views from the Masters concerning the fundamental nature of collection.

Collection, as the term is used in dressage, is the state of the horse in which it relieves its forehand by increasing the load on the engaged hindquarters...Carriage and responsiveness can be raised to their highest peaks, depending upon the degree of collection.

Waldemar Seunig *Horsemanship*

This succinct definition is remarkable in that it is *broadened* by what it does not say. It does not, for example, limit itself by mentioning length of stride, or speed of movement. Indeed, elsewhere in his book, Seunig emphasises this point:

In judging collection as a whole, one should be careful about taking a few external symptoms for the essentials, saying, 'The horse is collected *because* it yields its head and neck high.' The following description of a truly collected horse would be more nearly correct, 'This horse, collected as a result of correct action upon it, *cannot avoid* coming to the bit with a lifted forehand'. Waldemar Seunig *Horsemanship*

This broadening of the concept is continued by the academic General Decarpentry telling us first, that collection is by no means the sole preserve of the dressage arena, and second, that the type of collection to be sought when performing dressage has some things in common with the self-collection of the 'rogue' horse who is preparing himself for violent acts of defiance!

The Rassembler (collection) is the disposition of the horse's body which affects all of its parts and places each one in the best position to ensure the most efficient use of the energy produced by the efforts of the hind legs.

These efforts can have an immediate and special purpose, or can be a preparation for several eventual purposes.

The race horse before the start, the show jumper before going over an obstacle, the dressage horse before performing a courbette, all collect themselves, but the disposition of their body...is different in each case, and so is the direction in which their energy is spent ultimately.

But collection can also prepare for an output of energy that can be used for several purposes.

The 'rogue' who wants to resist and prepares himself to do so, adopts a general disposition that makes it possible for him to shy, to rear or to turn about, depending upon the vicissitudes of his struggle with the rider. He assumes an intermediate attitude that he can instantly modify. He also is collected, but his collection can serve several ends.

The kind of collection suited to academic equitation belongs to this last category, though it must not be confused of course with a preparation for resistance.

In the first place, it must ensure to the horse the maximum mobility in all directions and the ability to make rapid changes of speed. Furthermore, it must enable him, in answer to his rider's command, instantly to impart to his gaits the maximum elevation compatible with the length of stride that the rider wishes to maintain.   General Decarpentry *Academic Equitation*

Alfred Knopfhart echoes Decarpentry's view that collection is a state of preparedness that is relevant to all equestrian activities. He also makes the point that, while it is fundamentally important to the training process, it is not an end in itself:

Collection is often considered to be the sole purpose of dressage; it is not. Dressage education consists in cultivating to the utmost the physical and mental aptitudes of the horse, so that it can stay sound for as long as possible while satisfying the double requirement of speed and perfect tractability...

Collection is just a state of preparedness, of readiness to react rapidly in any direction that suits the rider; but it is a state that cannot be maintained for more than a short time without detriment to the soundness of body and mind of the horse. It is therefore just a means to an end. An educated rider should want to be able to collect a horse when hacking over difficult terrain, in critical situations in the hunting field, before tackling a high obstacle in show-jumping, or demanding a difficult movement in the manège.   Alfred Knopfhart *Fundamentals of Dressage*

The pragmatic, 'outdoor' collection, which is chiefly concerned with preparedness and balance, is described by Wilhelm Müseler in the following terms:

Ordinary working collection
By this position we understand the degree of collection at which

a horse is ridden across country. Any horse can go all his paces with more or less collection...Over ground with a lot of holes, across ploughed fields, or in the woods, a horse should always be collected in the same degree as in the school.

...i.e. in the appropriate degree of 'working collection'. Müseler compares this with what he describes as 'dressage collection', which is still not on the same level as that of the High School:

Dressage collection or dressage carriage
This position, as compared with the ordinary working position, requires an increased collection without, however, representing a *high degree* of collection and erection. The positions for ordinary work and for dressage are *relative* and involve relative degrees of collection, depending on the conformation of the horse.

Wilhelm Müseler *Riding Logic*

Seunig mentions both the 'state of preparedness' and 'dressage collection':

If *collection* is defined not merely as the bodily state in which the horse is best and most easily able to comply with the schooling requirements of the rider, it *signifies, when applied to all the branches of horsemanship, increased attentiveness and a readiness of execution that best corresponds to the particular object in view.*

In this sense collection is a relative term, comprising the readiness of the race horse at the start as well as that of the manège horse, flexing the springs of its hindquarters in the levade...   Waldemar Seunig *Horsemanship*

Erik Herbermann makes a distinction between the 'state of preparedness' and the specific qualities manifest in the collected gaits in the higher realms of dressage:

The term 'collection' is quite often mistakenly interchanged with 'on the aids'. Though the horse does indeed 'gather itself up' under the rider when it is put 'on the aids', there is an important difference between these two concepts...

To put a horse 'on the aids' means bringing it into a balanced, carrying, accepting state. *As a consequence* the horse yields at the poll, chews on the bit, and finds the correct head position. It is a 'cat-poised-to-pounce-on-a-mouse' state of willing readiness under the rider, and is the foundation for all correct work. A horse which is 'on the aids' is thereby prepared to do anything (depending, of course, on its individual level of training) which would include the extremes of the spectrum, both extension *and* collection in all three gaits.

Collection itself, however, is a state attained only after many years of patient, systematic, gymnastic work, which is made evident in a shorter, higher, rounder, *more active* stride. It is attained solely through a greater balancing of the horse on the hindquarters, *based on forward impulse* – and not merely by shortening the horse up from the front. The horse's motion must remain forward, fluid, and energetic, and must always continue to show the correct sequence of footfall in all gaits. The hallmark of true collection is a *clear lowering of the croup*, brought about by deeply bent, engaged quarters that carry more weight. This deep bending gives good collected work (despite its increased vigour) the distinction of uncanny quietness – a soft, elastic power – made possible through the flexing of the three major joints; hip, stifle and hock...this cannot be falsified and it requires willing participation and contribution from the horse.

Erik Herbermann   Dressage Formula

Herbermann's thoughts on the distinct use of terms lead us to consider other examples. During the middle years of the twentieth century, when Henry Wynmalen was riding and writing, many English riders used the term 'collected' in circumstances where we might now say 'on the aids', or 'between leg and hand'. In his books *Equitation* and *Dressage A Study of the Finer Points of Riding*, Wynmalen discusses and defines collection with reference to the Classical French terminology and the popular understanding of his era. In *Equitation*, his earlier work, he writes:

A horse which bends his head at the poll, drops his nose and flexes his jaw to the combined action of legs and hands is 'collected' and 'light in hand'. He is therefore easily controlled in all his paces and sufficiently collected for ordinary riding purposes. But to execute all the complicated school-movements with absolute accuracy, the intimate contact between rider and horse needs to be continuous and much closer than can be achieved by mere collection. The horse must be so perfectly collected, or 'gathered' (French: *rassemblé*), between the rider's legs and hands, that the rider can 'feel' the entire impulse of the animal resting on the tips of his fingers...It is only thus that the rider will be able to direct his mount as easily and as if he and the horse were one, and as if the horse responded to the directions of the rider's brain!

Henry Wynmalen *Equitation*

Later, in *Dressage A Study of the Finer Points of Riding*, he reprises his theme:

The literal translation of the French word *rassembler*, is the English word 'collection': unfortunately, the true implication of the two expressions is so vastly different that one just cannot use the one as a legitimate translation of the other.

The word 'collection', as understood in English, has a strictly limited meaning; it describes the 'attitude' or 'bearing' as assumed by the horse in certain of his exercises.

The word *rassembler*, used in the academic sense, has a far wider meaning; it embraces the entire demeanour of the horse in all his actions, the suppleness of his body, of his limbs and joints, the ease and generosity of his movements and, in particular, their rhythm and cadence; it embraces also the horse's absolute lightness…in effect, it embraces a high degree of all round perfection; it is at one and the same time the final object of the trainer's efforts and…when achieved, the crown upon his work.

Henry Wynmalen *Dressage A Study of the Finer Points of Riding*

The lightness of true, advanced collection, described by Wynmalen as 'absolute' is summed up by his French contemporary, André Jousseaume...

Lightness becomes perfect when collection is obtained.

André Jousseaume *Progressive Dressage*

...while Oliveira paints a picture of the consequent movement and its benefits:

The loins, hindquarters and hocks become flexible, the hocks push the horse's mass energetically ahead as the movement of the shoulders becomes free and graceful. The head and neck are placed high, and the lower jaw gives way at the lightest pressure of the rider's fingers.

The horse is so well balanced that the rider can ask any movement already taught with the minimum of effort, obtaining great promptness of execution.

Nuno Oliveira *Reflections on Equestrian Art*

Principles of Collection

Progression

It is one of the principles of Classical equitation that every-thing is done in due season; training is not only a layered process, it is also a process in which different aspects interlock to support each other. The Masters state clearly that this principle applies to collection, a quality which is inextricably linked to strength, suppleness, impulsion, submission and straightness.

Proper collection is the result of a long process of education through various stages that allows no tricks, no short cuts.

Alfred Knopfhart   *Fundamentals of Dressage*

The collected outline must be the inevitable consequence of total collection, that is, storing of energy…There are no special, mysterious aids for producing an elegant posture. The horse must first learn to obey all the aids and to move in a natural form before we can concentrate on producing the conventional outline of the highly collected horse.

Üdo Burger   *The Way to Perfect Horsemanship*

There are also warnings that premature attempts at collection will not just fail, but will actually backfire:

Premature collection either produces horses without impulsion or disobedient horses. The drive forward is the basis of all dressage training and cannot be established securely enough.

Gustav Steinbrecht *The Gymnasium of the Horse*

One result of such premature attempts at collection will be the opposite of our objective, for the horse, which has bent its hindquarters in a freer framework up to now and engaged them forward in accordance with the stage of its training and degree of development, will lose confidence and learn how to stiffen the joints of its hind legs to defend itself against the burden that it cannot yet carry.   Waldemar Seunig *Horsemanship*

These warnings are accompanied by counsels of patience:

For this collecting...it is...important that one should not make the deplorable mistake of trying to imitate the picture of a collected horse. The temptation is strong, especially if certain single points are over-valued. Collecting and erecting a horse must needs take a long time...The hind quarters (haunches) must first of all be physically trained and strengthened to make them fit to carry the load. If this process is hurried the horse will probably feel pains; soreness, stiffness, even lameness may result...

Wilhelm Müseler *Riding Logic*

At a later stage of its education, the horse will progressively also have to learn to collect itself, to flex its haunches and lighten its shoulders even more by lowering its croup. The flexion of haunches allows a 'relative elevation' of head and neck...

But first the horse must learn to move in horizontal equilibrium; the rider must never attempt to collect it before this horizontal equilibrium is perfectly confirmed and the strength of the hindquarters has been sufficiently developed to start asking them to carry a preponderance of weight. Once horizontal equilibrium is confirmed, collection, which involves increased loading of the hindquarters, can then be produced – but only very gradually – by the systematic practice of certain gymnastic lessons designed to develop their carrying capacity. If an impatient rider tried to gather his horse too soon he would provoke resistance; even a normally calm and willing horse can be driven to exasperation by excessive demands. It is impossible to obtain by force an engagement of hocks and flexion of haunches that would cause a horse pain.

Alfred Knopfhart *Fundamentals of Dressage*

Knopfhart also makes the point that patience must be accompanied by skill:

To teach a horse to collect itself willingly in obedience to the aids, the rider has to be very understanding and very patient; he must be able to feel the movements of the hind legs and to co-ordinate all his aids with great adroitness. Skill is necessary to get a horse to work and come on the bit without stiffening the poll or the jaw, when it is sent forward by the legs to the tactfully restraining and regulating hand. To obtain true collection is infinitely more difficult; the difficulty consisting principally of getting the horse to collect itself with ease and good grace in response to the most inconspicuous of aids.

Alfred Knopfhart *Fundamentals of Dressage*

Belasik echoes Knopfhart's thoughts...

All young horses need to engage their hind limbs actively in order to build the strength necessary for collection. Attempts to load the hind limbs without a proper forward stage of riding could easily cause the horse to develop evasions, since the horse would not yet be strong enough to collect correctly. A prematurely shortened step that is spasmodic in its rhythm, shallow in the flexion of the hock, hip, stifle, etc., or stiffly bouncy in the croup, can never be confused with true collection. True collection takes time, and has the great, elastic muscular control of a trained dancer. Paul Belasik *Dressage for the 21st Century*

...and points to the need for continuing vigilance in not demanding too much:

As some of the exercises become more and more physically and mentally demanding, the rider has to be...sure that the horse is strong enough to do what is required, and must then be careful not to fatigue the horse. If the horse is too weak, or too tired, it will be unable to perform the exercise correctly, for instance, with deep-set haunches. Consequently, the horse may be more or less obliged to 'cheat' in the exercise. I think this is one of the most common sources of faulty movements later on.

Paul Belasik *Dressage for the 21st Century*

This need to ensure sufficient strength and suppleness is underlined by Seunig:

An increased degree of collection can be achieved only when the suppleness and carrying capacity of the hindquarters allow the rider to place a heavier burden upon them.

Waldemar Seunig *Horsemanship*

Excessive demands would, of course, be likely causes for the tension and resistances which are proscribed in this work:

Essential to collection...is the complete lack of resistances, as well as the maintenance of superior impulsion, and absolute submission. Nuno Oliveira *Reflections on Equestrian Art*

In the more advanced education of the horse, when it has to learn to move in collection...its submission cannot be obtained if it does not ease all tension unnecessary to the execution of the movement (a rigid body cannot be compacted into a small frame). Suppleness is always a requisite of good work...

Alfred Knopfhart *Fundamentals of Dressage*

A major factor in assessing what are reasonable demands is the individual horse's aptitude:

Not all horses can achieve the same degree of collection...What constitutes the maximum physical and psychological collection for sluggish horses of poor conformation may be mere ordinary riding posture for born riding horses.

Waldemar Seunig *Horsemanship*

The degree of collection that can be expected depends on the aptitude and level of education of the horse. It always depends, in any case, on progressive education, and the sort of collection that can be demanded of an advanced dressage horse is very different from the collection that can be obtained from a six-year-old at elementary or medium level...

Alfred Knopfhart *Fundamentals of Dressage*

However, Knopfhart adds the point that:

Although the degree of collection attainable varies according to the conformation and temperament of the individual horse...the progressive work towards collection is the same for all horses.

Alfred Knopfhart *Fundamentals of Dressage*

The progression towards collection is summarised by d'Endrödy:

The complete process of collection is composed of the following phases (in the order in which they should be executed):

the loosening exercise;

the establishment of the mental and physical contact;

the regulation of the horse's motion;

the creation of liveliness, the performance of distinct alterations within certain paces, changes of paces, and the execution of rein-back movements;

the increase of suppleness by practising some short turns and movements on two tracks.

These are the introductory exercises which pave the way for collection. If they are carried out properly, they will already create a certain degree of collection...

Lt. Col. A.L. d'Endrödy *Give Your Horse a Chance*

With the rider's role being summed up by Steinbrecht:

The understanding trainer, gifted with a well developed rider's intuition, will soon sense from the horse's behavior how much he must load the hindquarters to bring the horse into balance, which will then be expressed by a beautiful, natural elevation of head and neck, by free, elastic movements of the forelegs from the shoulders, and by strong, determined follow-up of the hindquarters. He will select the means of achieving this goal with consideration for his horse's conformation, temperament and age. The more careful he is in this selection, the faster he will reach his goal...Never forget that dressage training should be controlled gymnastics, not forced exercises, and that the horse's body should not be pressed all at once into the desired mold, but should gradually be enabled to take on this shape without force.

Gustav Steinbrecht *The Gymnasium of the Horse*

Mechanics

Collection is not, by any means, an entirely mechanical process. It requires, for example, a good deal of 'feel', or finesse from the rider, and an underlying forward impulse, coupled with ready compliance from the horse. Indeed, Richard Wätjen makes the point that...

The collection and proper head carriage of a well-trained horse cannot be mechanically determined, but must always be adapted to the conformation and individuality of each horse...

Richard Wätjen *Dressage Riding*

That said, collection is essentially a biomechanical adjustment of the horse's movement, and it is highly unlikely that the adjustments will be made correctly unless the basic mechanics are understood.

As will become evident from the Masters' writings, one of the greatest faults in seeking collection is an over-reliance on the reins. It is, however, a *prerequisite* of seeking collection that the horse fully accepts the bit. The basic progression is explained by Wynmalen, who translates the French terminology into the English terminology of his era:

The first step is the attainment of a measure of acceptance of the bit, characterised by flexions of the jaw, accompanied by a measure of flexion at the poll, resulting in a measure of correct head carriage. It is what the French call *le ramener*...done properly...we might perhaps call it 'collection of the first degree'...the accent is on 'done properly', namely by riding the horse forward, towards his head, and not by pulling the horse's head back towards his body…

We are then ready to continue working towards the achievement of 'collection' in the English sense, which I would like to call 'collection in the second degree' and which is known in French as *la mise en main* meaning the horse which 'goes in hand'. The accent is on 'goes': the horse goes forward freely, with a perfectly balanced, energetic stride, with a nice soft pressure on the rein; the hocks are active and the shoulders move freely…

Henry Wynmalen *Dressage A Study of the Finer Points of Riding*

The ramener and its attainment are analysed by Decarpentry…

The Ramener is the closing of the angle of the head with the neck, the poll remaining the highest point of the latter.

The Ramener is said to be *complete* when the nose reaches the vertical; if the nose comes behind the vertical, the horse is no longer 'ramené', he is overbent.

The Ramener can be achieved by drawing the head towards the body or by pushing the body towards the head, or by combining both movements…

But the intrinsic advantages of the Ramener are accompanied by serious drawbacks when it is obtained by drawing the head and neck towards the trunk, because the Ramener then necessarily communicates this backward movement to the trunk itself…whereas the whole progression of dressage aims at driving the horse forward into the opposite attitude of collection.

…who goes on to say:

…the trainer will try to obtain the Ramener by practising variations of speed and transitions, but always without destroying the forward movement.

General Decarpentry *Academic Equitation*

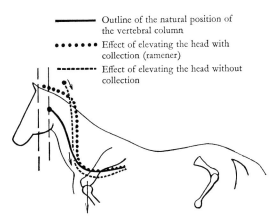

———— Outline of the natural position of
the vertebral column

• • • • • • Effect of elevating the head with
collection (ramener)

- - - - - - - Effect of elevating the head without
collection

Lifting of the Neck

Diagram of vertebral column in natural position

Effect of elevation
without Ramener

Effect of elevation
with Ramener

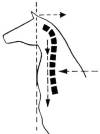

WITHOUT RAMENER

—the poll is drawn backwards
—the chain of cervical vertebrae
is compressed downwards
—It flexes forwards at the lower part,
thus causing a ewe-neck
(Pigeon Throat).

WITH RAMENER

The poll is advanced
or (in front of the perpendicular)
The vertebrae are curved and
stretched correctly from
the bottom upwards.
The neck is correctly carried
from the base upwards.

*Diagrams showing the effects of elevating the head and neck with and
without ramener, from General Decarpentry's* Academic Equitation.

L'Hotte points out that the position of the horse's head in ramener is, in effect, a subsidiary consequence of submission of the jaw. He also makes the point that suppleness (or tension) in one part of the body will have a consequential effect upon other parts:

The *ramener*, as it is understood in high equitation, has little to do with the position of the horse's head. It lies, first of all, in the submission of the jaw which is the first joint that receives the effect of the hand. If this joint responds with softness to the action that solicits its play, it will bring about the flexibility of the neck and provoke the suppleness of the other joints due to the instinctive correlation that exists between all muscular contractions. If, on the other hand, the jaw resists or refuses to be mobilized, then there is no lightness; it is natural that resistances will support each other and have many echoes. Thus, in Classical equitation what the *ramener* represents is less an unchanging position of the head, but, rather, a general condition of the submission and pliancy of all the joints and muscles.

Alexis-François L'Hotte *Questions Équestres* (in *Alexis-François L'Hotte The Quest For Lightness in Equitation*, by Hilda Nelson)

Whereas L'Hotte focuses on flexion of the jaw, Kurt Albrecht looks to the poll, but makes similar points to L'Hotte in relating this localised flexion to overall demeanour, activity and carriage:

Far too many riders continue to confuse collection and submission of the poll and neglect to cultivate the suppleness of the poll until they start working on the collected gaits.

Direct flexion at the poll may be difficult for some horses either because of unfavourable conformation of the first two cervical vertebrae or because of the shape of the mandible and resulting compression of the parotid glands. Such disadvantages have to be neutralized as soon as possible…

However most resistances to flexion of the poll stem from the stiffness or weakness of the hindquarters rather than from the conformation of the mandible or the upper cervical vertebrae and it is impossible to overcome resistance if its actual source is wrongly identified. Stiffening of the poll rooted in stiffness of the hind joints cannot be corrected by the hand.

Similarly, pliancy of the poll has to go hand-in-hand with a corresponding activity of the hindquarters. Hence one should not demand utmost flexion of the poll before the muscles of the hindquarters have acquired sufficient strength and elasticity. Trying to impose an ideal head position with the reins alone, without consideration of the engagement of the hind limbs, usually results in dangerously exaggerated bridling or overbending, that is to say a break in the curve of the neck behind the two first vertebrae that form the poll. Both faults shorten the frame in a useless manner and prevent effective control of the hindquarters.

Flexion of the poll and compacting of the frame has to be the *result* of impulsion; it has to come from behind...

Kurt Albrecht *Principles of Dressage*

Oliveira also highlights the relationship that should exist between the ramener and the engagement of the hindquarters...

The 'ramener', that is, the placing of the horse's neck and head, should always be in proportion to the degree of engagement of the hind legs...

Nuno Oliveira *Notes and Reminiscences of a Portuguese Rider*

...his point being echoed by Wynmalen:

...whatever the head carriage may look like, it can be of no value unless it is based on increased energy of the quarters, resulting in free and improved forward movement.

Henry Wynmalen *Dressage A Study of the Finer Points of Riding*

While Steinbrecht has a highly pragmatic observation:

If the rider wants to move the weight from the forehand to the rear, he must have a support onto which he can move the weight so that, after being lifted...it will not fall back onto its former point of support, namely the forelegs. The proper supports, however, can only be the stronger hind legs...It is therefore quite a useless and unnatural undertaking if...riders attempt to force their horses' heads and necks into an elevated position before they are able to bring the hind legs under correspondingly with their legs. They will be forced to carry the lifted weight themselves, that is, continuously support it with their hands. They will not transfer the weight to the hindquarters but only unnaturally bend their horses' backs.

Waldemar Seunig's own drawing of cramped and incorrect movement from The Essence of Horsemanship.

Putting the weight on the hindquarters, in other words, collecting the horse, must therefore begin from the back in that, by doubled activity and attentiveness on the part of his legs, the rider stimulates the hind legs to lively and deliberate movement.

Gustav Steinbrecht *The Gymnasium of the Horse*

It seems hardly surprising, therefore, that it is the engagement of the hindquarters which is identified by L'Hotte as the defining characteristic of rassembler – the state of full collection:

The *rassembler*, characterized by the flexibility of the haunches which includes the engagement of the hocks under the mass; the different degrees of engagement in proportion to the nature of the movement sought.

Alexis-François L'Hotte *Questions Équestres* (in *Alexis-François L'Hotte The Quest For Lightness in Equitation*, by Hilda Nelson)

So, although in their discussion of collection the Masters may start by examining acceptance of the bit and head carriage, the field of study quickly expands to include the action of the hindquarters. As Wynmalen explains, it is by correctly influencing both ends of the horse that the rider works towards collection:

The basic principle of that work is...that of gradually increasing the action of the hocks to engage just a little further under the body; it implies the shortening of the base whereon the horse moves just a little; the horse brings his rump and quarters a little nearer to his head; to do so, the horse must of necessity lower his quarters a fraction, resulting in a relatively higher position of the forehand.

...It must be clearly understood that in all the work undertaken to reach the *mise en main* or 'collected movement' we must pursue, and cannot do other than pursue, two aims simultaneously: that of increasing the energy of the horse's action on a shorter base and that of creating a happy mouth; the two…are inseparable.

Henry Wynmalen *Dressage A Study of the Finer Points of Riding*

Commenting further on shortening the base of support, Wynmalen adds:

We are aiming, in this work, at shortening the base whereon the horse moves…Which is far from simple. It cannot be done without an immense increase in the pliability and suppleness of all the horse's muscles and…joints. That necessitates…a course of carefully thought out and methodically applied gymnastic exercises…

It will be understood that the horse's ability to shorten his base in movement…can only develop gradually and in precise measure wherein the pliability of his muscles and joints increases. The horse will be ready enough to try and execute his rider's demands…in accordance with his physical ability. Beyond that, he obviously cannot go; so, if forced beyond his physical powers, he can do no other than take evading action; he does that by going sideways, 'traversing himself'.

Henry Wynmalen *Dressage A Study of the Finer Points of Riding*

Wynmalen's emphasis upon increasing pliability and suppleness suggests that shortening the base of support is not the same thing as 'contraction'. Knopfhart elaborates upon this point:

In collection, all the muscles of the horse's locomotor system have to work in particularly close co-operation not only to produce movement but also to support an abnormal proportion of weight and to allow the elevation of the forehand. The visible signs of collection are not only the elevated carriage of head and neck, the regularity and liveliness of the steps but also, and especially, the visible activity of the back muscles which must act like springs strongly tensioned to support the weight of the rider and of the neck and head of the horse while simultaneously co-ordinating the movements of the fore and hind limbs. The whole body of the horse gives the appearance of being contracted in a smaller frame, but in reality as a result of correct bridling and of a shortened base of support, the back becomes more convex and therefore longer, stronger and more elastic.

Alfred Knopfhart *Fundamentals of Dressage*

While Seunig observes:

Correct collection requires that the back be stretched considerably. This increased elastic tension is produced by having the croup and buttock muscles of the engaged hindquarters exert a stronger pull downwards and backwards upon the muscles of the back connected to them...Another contributing factor is the tension of the back muscles in the opposite direction produced via the ligamentum nuchae owing to the extension of the head and neck forward and upward. This elastic tension, which is produced by the lively, energetic gait...is wholly unrelated to convulsive tightness...   Waldemar Seunig *Horsemanship*

Burger, also commenting on the elastic tension of the topline, emphasises that correct arching will be achieved only by the rider whose chief focus is upon the hindquarters, rather than the head:

The arching of the topline is the result of a constant tension of the muscles of the topline, an elastic tension…Similarly, the tension of the reins must be constant. However, the arching of the neck is useless to a rider who cannot also command the arching of the back by determining the swinging of the hindlegs. When the bow behind the saddle is firmly braced, as in collection, the same tension of muscles is continued through the back muscles to the neck, which is then naturally elevated and arched by intrinsic forces...In the absence of overall elastic muscular tension and satisfactory impulsion, the rein effects stop at the saddle; though the mouth, the poll and the neck yield, the horse is shortened only in his neck and overbends. He can also resist by refusing to engage his hindquarters...

Therefore collection cannot be obtained by shortening the reins and pulling with the arms; the parades are not properly an activity of the hands but rather a change of distribution of the rider's weight, which he executes by imperceptibly drawing himself taller, without leaning backward.

Üdo Burger   The Way to Perfect Horsemanship

In similar vein, d'Endrödy states...

The higher the degree of the collection, the closer are these points [**mouth and hocks**] to each other. This shift in their position, however, must be achieved by pushing the hocks more and more forward to the mouth and by no means by pulling the mouth nearer to the hocks.

...adding:

The proper bearing of the horse must come as a result of the exercises which are designed to collect it...It is important to note that the rider cannot hasten the improvement of the neck-carriage by shortening the reins, but must adapt the length of the reins to the *horse's* improvement. The difference between following and initiating the shortening process is considerable. It is bad practice not to follow this natural improvement, but it is even worse when the rider tries to enforce it arbitrarily by shortening the reins. From such an attempt originates the greatest fault in riding, namely the forced compression of the horse.

Lt. Col. A.L. d'Endrödy   Give Your Horse a Chance

The contribution of various exercises towards obtaining collection is also mentioned by Müseler. However, he also introduces a contentious note by discussing the issue of direct erection (elevation) of the forehand:

The school horse...especially if he is to do high school work, must use his hind legs, not so much for propulsion as for carrying purposes, and they must therefore be made to step well forward and under the centre of gravity...

Collection is obtained partly by special exercises serving this particular purpose, such as bending the hocks, side-stepping and shoulder-in, and partly by the whole of the training through which the horse is put, as well as by every single half-halt.

Through this kind of work the...hind quarters become lower, the hind legs are busier and more energetic...

As a consequence of the lowering of the hind quarters the relieved forehand is automatically raised or erected. The front legs show a higher and prouder action, and at the same time the stride becomes shorter (relative erection). This (relative) erection can be increased through active influences by raising the neck and head a little higher, while at the same time energetically driving forward with back and legs (direct erection). It is important, however, that the driving influences predominate, otherwise the natural consequence of such erection is a hollow back in the horse. 　　　　Wilhelm Müseler *Riding Logic*

As will be clear from this passage, direct elevation entails intervention from the rider in the form of distinct rein effects. It is also clear that Müseler warns about the potential dangers of this technique, and counsels great discretion. He is by no means the only authority to mention direct elevation – Seunig, for example, writes:

This (relative) raising becomes a direct or active raising at the moment in which the hand through light aids on the reins improves the overall posture of the horse. The indicating rein aids are necessary because most horses lack an innate motivation to offer more than a relative raising of the forehand; maybe there are some who are especially outgoing and take it as their happy duty to collect themselves.

These comments are, however, ringed by caveats...

The raising of the forehand is a characteristic and a result of collection. It is the by-product, not in itself the aim, of the dressage training. It comprises a developing elevation of poll, neck and withers out of the shoulders as a result of a lowering of the flexed hindquarters and the passively resisting rein...

The degree of raising of the forehand cannot be described by any schematic formula. It is dependent on the rideability, the conformation, and the temperament of each individual horse, and is a function of the greater or lesser engagement of the haunches. The raising of the forehand will have been achieved in its appropriate degree if the horse in complete suppleness moves with animation through the poll and onto the bit.

Waldemar Seunig *The Essence of Horsemanship*

...and in *Horsemanship*, he writes:

Lifting the forehand is a consequence of the lowering of the hindquarters produced by their greater engagement. It is an indication and a consequence of collection. In a correctly collected horse the croup and buttock muscles of the engaged hindquarters exert a powerful tug downwards and backwards upon the muscles of the back connected to them, thus lifting the chest and neck vertebrae...and taking some of the load off the forehand...Lifting the forehand is relative so long as it is merely a consequence of the lowered hindquarters and of the passively holding reins...

Correct head carriage and lifting of the forehand are not major goals of dressage but rather accompaniments and consequences of proper work. As such, like the hands of a clock keeping correct time, they tell the expert that the timing and the locomotion of the horse are in order.

But one who does not possess very unusual experience and a trained eye should never try to concentrate upon head and neck alone in judging head carriage and the lift of the forehand. Only observation of the entire horse, of its carriage and especially its gait, this incorruptible evidence of honest work, will be able to prove unmistakably that they are correct.

Waldemar Seunig *Horsemanship*

The dangers of overemphasising direct elevation are described frankly by Podhajsky. In his book, *My Horse, My Teachers,* he relates the salutary lesson learnt with his horse, Otto, who subsequently became a top performer and was reserve horse at the 1936 Olympics:

Subconsciously, I allowed Otto a lower position of his head and neck than my other horses had adopted and heard a good amount of criticism from the older rider-comrades. Finally I gave in and tried to raise Otto's head and neck and give him a more elevated position. With the result that he who had been so willing began to be resistant. In spite of his good paces he lost all impulsion, his reluctance grew, and at last he refused to go forward altogether. In excitement he raised his head too high and came above the bit. If I tried to ride him forward energetically he pressed himself against my pushing aids and finally rose straight up on his hind legs...The bitter experience with Otto taught me that the rider must never give more elevation to his horse than is allowed by his conformation and the stage of his training and by no means by taking his head and neck up. Otto was young and in spite of the fact that he looked to be a strong horse, he had a weak back...When I raised his head and neck his back began to ache and induced him to defend himself...After this disaster I allowed him time for his development and tried to obtain the elevation in the natural way...by increased action of his hindquarters. Now his back was well arched and able to carry the rider. He felt no discomfort...and there was no reason for resistance...The work with him and the failure I suffered in its beginning taught me to turn away once and forever from forced training and to give true measure to the factor of time.

Alois Podhajsky My Horses, My Teachers

It is evident that this experience had a profound effect upon Podhajsky:

Collection must be obtained by pushing the hindquarters towards the reins, which remain applied. The compression...of the horse must be produced by pushing forwards from behind and not by pulling back with the reins. The latter would create an incorrect collection and the hind feet of the horse would not track up to the forefeet. Only when collection is obtained from rear to front will the horse step under the body with his hind legs in such a way that the rider can feel it in the reins...

One of the most important principles of horsemanship is that the horse must never be worked from front to rear but always from behind forward. This principle must become an irrevocable rule...The rider must beware of achieving an apparently good position with the reins and neglecting impulsion and, above all, the action of the horse. An apparently correct position reached by incorrect methods will lead to disappointment and difficulties...Only if the collection and contact are reached by impulsive action will they last and continue through the most difficult exercises.

Alois Podhajsky *The Complete Training of Horse and Rider*

While Podhajsky admits to error, and authorities such as Müseler and Seunig advise great caution in attempting active elevation, there were those who actively advocated it as a means of lowering the hindquarters, envisaging the horse almost as a seesaw. In the following passage, Decarpentry points out the flaws in their theory. He also embraces L'Hotte's views on the interrelationship of true ramener with the rest of the body, points out that the lowering and engagement of the haunches is the fundamental aim and stresses the need to prepare the hindquarters properly:

It is frequently asserted that the lifting of the neck without Ramener necessarily unloads the forehand and loads the hind-quarters. The spine being held to act as the arm of a pair of scales, with its fulcrum situated...in the region of the withers.

Granted, if the spine were rigid and the famous fixed point...really existed.

But it does not exist, because the horse has not got a collar bone...In the horse, this joint with the forelegs does not exist. This fulcrum...which would allow the spine to act as the arm of a pair of scales is purely imaginary.

The spine of the horse, through the intermediary of the thorax to which it is joined, lies between the two shoulders in a kind of cradle constituted of muscles and cartilage. This cradle is neither rigid nor of fixed shape, it has the elasticity common to all muscular tissue...

If one lifts the neck bodily its lower part sinks in the cradle, the withers sink between the shoulders, and the spine, behind the withers, sinks under the saddle.

The weight supposedly transferred to the hind-quarters...in fact simply remains on the forehand – whilst the back caves in. The lower part of the neck is thrown out: the horse becomes 'pigeon-throated'...

The whole situation is different, if this elevation is accompanied by a suitable Ramener. The poll moves forward to align itself vertically with the nose, the first vertebrae, axis and atlas, move from back to front...the succeeding ones are drawn up because they are joined to the others which pull them and from bottom to top they draw with them the rest of the neck which therefore can no longer sink between the shoulders.

Furthermore, all the other muscles of the neck which were slackened when the head was lifted without Ramener now are tensed and their tension is communicated to the muscles of the back, the tension of which in turn prevents the sinking of the rib-cage.

It is clear that forcibly pulling up the neck only, with the head in a horizontal position, produces misleading results in the first place, and difficulties in the end.

Furthermore, the loins as well as all the joints of the hind-quarters must be adequately prepared by proper gymnastics for the true burden imposed upon them by the lifting of the neck in the position of the Ramener. Otherwise, they lose their activity and their suppleness.

The elevation of the neck must therefore be achieved very progressively...as all the joints of the hind-quarters become better capable of flexing they facilitate the lowering of the quarters.

It is not the elevation of the neck, but the lowering of the haunches that is the aim to pursue. Lifting the neck is only a part of the whole work that contributes to the end...

Finally, it must be realised that lifting the neck produces the intended result only if it remains in position *without the support of the rider's hands*...

So long as the horse keeps his neck lifted only by more or less propping himself on the rider's hands...the horse is not 'lifted in front'.

This elevation can be considered to be achieved and effectual when the horse can hold it by his own effort without relying at all on the assistance of the rider whose hands must remain in their normal place...   General Decarpentry *Academic Equitation*

Focusing on the lowering of the haunches and the consequential relative elevation of the forehand, Knopfhart warns of the dangers of active elevation:

The flexion of the haunches produces a lowering of the croup and compels the hind legs to function more in the capacity of flexible props than propelling levers; this automatically lightens and elevates the forehand. The elevation of the forehand must be a 'relative' elevation, rather than an 'active' elevation i.e. forced holding up of the head and neck by the reins. The degree of elevation of the forehand depends very much on the horse's conformation, especially on the articulation of neck and back. Active elevation of the neck presses the base of the neck down between the shoulders, stiffens the horse's back, hinders the engagement of the hindquarters and breaks the horse into two unrelated parts. When the rider relaxes the strong hold on the reins, instead of lengthening its stride, the horse comes above the bit and hurries.

He is entirely dismissive of crude attempts to use the neck as a lever...

Nothing can be more dangerous than using the reins to utilize the neck as a lever to enforce the flexion of haunches if the muscles of the back and hindquarters are still too weak. Active elevation of the neck produces such painful pressure on the cervical vertebrae that any horse will defend itself instinctively by rigidly tensing the muscles of its back or slackening them completely...

Tugging at the reins to enforce collection is not only ugly, but also useless and just a sign of stiffened hind joints. Besides which it is a serious tactical error, because it makes it strikingly obvious even to a distantly situated and not very attentive observer that the horse is either lacking in submission to the leg aid or incapable of carrying enough weight on its hind legs.

...but discusses the role of the rider's hands in context:

Correct elevation of the neck and lightening of the forehand depend entirely on sufficient engagement of the hindquarters. It may be necessary to use the hands frequently but only to remind the horse that it must continue to hold up its neck by its own force. The role of the legs is even more important; they must ensure that the hind feet step sufficiently forward to allow the hindquarters to support enough weight. This is an absolute condition of lightness...Collection can only be obtained by driving the whole mass of the horse 'from behind' and cannot be appraised by observing only the position of head and neck.

Alfred Knopfhart Fundamentals of Dressage

The combination of forward-driving aids combined with mainly passive hands is also mentioned by Seunig. In a passage describing the progress towards obtaining collection, he writes:

Once this vigorous step [active engagement] is assured in a state of suppleness, the rider can begin to employ his forward-driving seat control to collect the horse, driving with the small of his back, passively sustaining with his hands the increased impulsion that the seat has contributed to them and – after the resultant yielding of the horse – making sure that this impulsion persists and can be converted into engagement and collection.

Waldemar Seunig *Horsemanship*

Jousseaume also points to the need for great sensitivity in the use of the hands...

...it is indispensable that the impulsion given by the legs, with the goal of engaging the hindquarters, be received by an extremely sensitive hand... André Jousseaume *Progressive Dressage*

...while Steinbrecht states that stiff, heavy-handed riders are doomed to failure in their misdirected efforts to obtain collection:

The rider should not try to put the load on the hindquarters primarily with his hands. Through forward driving aids, he must cause the hind legs to step more underneath the weight and take on the load themselves...The elevation of the forehand then comes automatically, the more the hindquarters are lowered and bent.

This rule is often disregarded, particularly by riders who, because their body is too stiff, have dead legs and therefore always tend to overcome this drawback by increased activity of their hands. Since under such riders, the insufficiently stimulated hind legs do not step far enough underneath the load to be truly bent, the activity of their hands is unsuccessful; they merely interfere with the horse's movement and thus deprive themselves of the only means for attaining the desired goal. Thrust cannot be regulated if none exists, and the horse cannot learn to move correctly if it does not move.

Gustav Steinbrecht *The Gymnasium of the Horse*

Wätjen, also, proscribes abuses of the rein aids and focuses on correct use of the seat and back...

The horse must carry itself by its own impulsion, without seeking support from the rider's hand. Shortening the neck should be strictly avoided as it deprives the horse of its natural impulsion and free forward movement...

A forced collection is highly detrimental, as it prevents the horse from engaging its hocks and hindquarters in the correct manner...

In obtaining collection the greatest part is played by the rider's seat; his braced back must form an unchangeable, supple, and yet firm connection with the horse's back. His hands must be steady and supple, offering the required resistance so that the animating aids are checked by the bit, and thus represent a limited resistance, by which the horse...is collected...By means of the driving aids the horse is collected from the rear to the front. This collection must be supplemented and maintained again and again by riding straight on and freely forward. In each pace...the urge to ride forward must predominate.

...dismissing attempts to 'collect' the horse by artificial means...

There is no doubt of the bad consequences which follow a forced, unnatural collection gained by artificial means (mainly running reins) which one so often observes. As a result of this excessive pressure of the bit on the jaw, the horse is more or less forced to bend its neck and to adopt a head position which is no way in harmony with the engagement of the hind-quarters. The consequence of continuing to ride in this manner is, obviously, a bad head carriage. The horse bends at the neck and is *not* bent at the poll, thus making...the proper influence of the hind-quarters – the forward drive from behind, through the horse, to the bit – impossible. Richard Wätjen *Dressage Riding*

...a practice which is also condemned by d'Endrödy:

The great distinction of the horse's general appearance makes a striking impression on riders who neglect the serious work required to produce it. Instead, these riders will use various artificial measures in an attempt to impose upon their horses a bearing which somehow resembles that of an animal which is collected. This kind of interference must be condemned! Such measures neither increase nor preserve the energy of the horse, but, on the contrary, cause useless fidgetings which waste its power.

The basic principle which should govern the construction of the collecting procedure is that the span desired in the horse's spring system must be created by the *animal itself,* using the inherent collecting power of its motion; the rider's contribution is to inspire the animal for the performance of the necessary motion... Lt. Col. A.L. d'Endrödy *Give Your Horse a Chance*

Herbermann and Schramm voice their disapproval of all 'quick-fix' methods, whether artificial or otherwise:

The use of 'quick-fix' methods to achieve unmerited collection is probably one of the most common causes of resistances, disharmony, and lameness in the horse.

Erik Herbermann *Dressage Formula*

Bridle-lameness is an acquired, rider-produced vice, a trick discovered by a horse to evade a heavy-handed rider's attempts to obtain the flexion of the poll; the horse has learnt that it can avoid collection by stepping short with one hindleg...The irregularity often develops when a horse is made to perform certain dressage movements before it has learnt to go forwards without being constricted by severe hands...In fact the bridle-lame horse is vascillating [sic] between a longing to hurry and go above the bit, and reluctance to go forward...

Discussing this fault with specific reference to the trot, Schramm adds...

The trot...is also impure if a hindfoot or a forefoot impact later than its diagonal opposite. Usually this happens when a rider has attempted to enforce collection before sufficiently developing the carrying capacity of the hindlegs, or has tried to lighten the forehand by actively elevating the neck, thus preventing the...activity of the back muscles and breaking the connection between hindquarters and mouth.

Ulrik Schramm *The Undisciplined Horse*

Others also comment on impure movement and loss of activity:

The animal is inclined to give up its collection and bearing quite suddenly when it loses its liveliness and lags behind with the quarters. The manifestation of this deficiency is a tossing of the head and neck or a hard, stiff pushing against the bit. The...rider should act with the aim of preserving the *obedience* (mental contact and submission) of the horse, but not with the direct intention to safeguard the *shape* of its deportment, which is only one of the physical manifestations of its obedience.

Lt. Col. A.L. d'Endrödy *Give Your Horse a Chance*

It is easy to see that a horse has been asked for collection beyond its capacity if it drags its hind legs, moves too slowly or too hurriedly, hunches or hollows its back, overbends in the neck, or sets its poll and its mouth. Alternately, it may go with a lifted croup, erratically swinging hind legs, on too long a rein, with its nose poked and its neck stiffened.

Alfred Knopfhart *Fundamentals of Dressage*

Knopfhart goes on to say:

If gait and carriage have suffered as a consequence of premature efforts to produce collection, there is no other remedy than retreat to the level at which the fault started...one may have to go back a long way but there is no choice.

It is often because the horse has not been sufficiently suppled and straightened in the previous stages of its education that it resists attempts to teach it collection. One should never attempt to obtain any measure of collection before a horse has learnt to engage both its hind legs equally in all three medium gaits and in transitions.   Alfred Knopfhart *Fundamentals of Dressage*

Burger also focuses on the need to develop the hindquarters, and explains how resistances will arise if the undeveloped horse is punished by his own obedience:

Obtaining collection is certainly the greatest difficulty of dressage and the origin of the difficulty is invariably the weakness of the hindquarters. Extreme flexion of the hocks is tiring and soon produces soreness of muscles. If the horse is obedient and the rider unsympathetic, every step in collection will punish the horse for his obedience. Eventually, to obtain relief, the horse must straighten his hocks, but then he is no longer submissive. For him, it is much easier, much less effort, to fight the rider's hands than to yield to the compression of the hind joints.
                    Üdo Burger *The Way to Perfect Horsemanship*

Like Burger, Belasik denies neither the difficulty of obtaining true collection, nor the need to do so by correct means:

Collection is still the concept of rebalancing weight toward the hind legs, thereby lightening the forehand. That this is rarely done, or is very difficult to accomplish, is no reason to accept less...Engagement of the haunches has to be based on impulsive, forward riding with a correct seat, otherwise attempts at collection present a real danger of hollowing the horse's back and disengaging the hind legs.

Paul Belasik *Dressage for the 21st Century*

Summarising the qualities of correct collection, Wynmalen emphasises the fundamental need for impulsion...

We may qualify as correctly collected...the horse that goes forward with energy (impulsion), well off his hocks, well up to his bit, with a correct head position, flexed at the poll, happy in his mouth and straight. If any of the factors here mentioned are missing, collection has not been fully achieved. We frequently see horses presented in collected gaits which lack all real impulsion and brilliance; their movements are merely slow and, in a sense, extinguished; such horses are not 'collected'...

Henry Wynmalen *Dressage A Study of the Finer Points of Riding*

...and stresses the ultimate value of free forward movement:

Throughout our training of the riding horse it is our object to attain lightness in front through increased activity of the quarters; but lightness alone is of no value unless we maintain ...and improve, free and generous forward movement...In fact, if we had to choose between the two, the free forward movement would be the more important quality.

Henry Wynmalen *Dressage A Study of the Finer Points of Riding*

While the importance of a continuous forward impulse is also stressed by other authorities:

Whoever knows to maintain the forward drive during collecting work and to always correctly adjust forehand and hindquarters relative to one another, will never be seriously at a loss for action.   Gustav Steinbrecht *The Gymnasium of the Horse*

The collected paces by their regularity, rhythm, and liveliness must be the image of controlled force. Impulsion must be seen in collection as well as in the immediate extension.

Alois Podhajsky *The Complete Training of Horse and Rider*

To collect a horse means creating suppleness and lightness...A proof of a true collection is a free, unconstrained and energetic forward movement...   Richard Wätjen *Dressage Riding*

Collection and Straightness

As is evident from the Masters' writings, collection is closely linked to several important facets of training. Indeed, its links with strength, impulsion and submission are so close that these qualities are almost inevitably mentioned whenever collection is discussed. The same is probably true of suppleness in its longitudinal form. However, the qualities of lateral suppleness and straightness – whilst highly significant – seem often to be addressed at one remove.

It is a key requirement of true collection that both hind limbs carry an equal load – and this can occur only if the horse is straight. Therefore, in the detail of their writings, the Masters place great emphasis on the attainment of suppleness and straightness. Here are a few examples of their thoughts.

Correct collection will be possible only when the horse is straight, balanced, and in contact with the bit.

Alois Podhajsky *The Complete Training of Horse and Rider*

Only if the horse is totally straight, perfectly light to the hand...is 3rd degree collection possible.

André Jousseaume *Progressive Dressage*

It is a peculiarity of all vertebrates to proceed in a more or less serpentine manner. At the walk the extent of the spinal movements are particularly easy to observe and to feel with long-backed, long-striding horses. In order to obtain collection it is necessary to stabilize the vertebral column, to reduce the sideways movement as much as possible...

True collection can only be achieved by very gradually building up the horse's ability to move energetically and perfectly regularly in short steps but with great impulsion, on very flexed, very elastic hind joints...It must be made so supple by appropriate gymnastic exercises that it can be incurvated as easily to one side as the other... Alfred Knopfhart *Fundamentals of Dressage*

Let us repeat that the two groups of muscles lying on either side of the spinal column, which pulsate elastically rather than convulsively, must work quite uniformly along a straight line and on a single track. If they do not do so, the horse becomes crooked, with its legs not carrying an equal load on both sides, and we get the *impure* gait in all its variants. Waldemar Seunig *Horsemanship*

The important role of lateral work is mentioned by Albrecht...

One should never forget that the lateral movements were designed to help strengthen the hind legs with a view to their role in collection. Kurt Albrecht *Principles of Dressage*

...and also by Seunig, who points to the close links between various aspects of training:

Correct riding on two tracks requires a certain degree of collection, which is advanced further by two-track exercise. It is quite wrong, however, to assume that a horse that cannot be collected will learn collection by work on two tracks. Such a horse, which is not yet ready to work on two tracks, would merely throw more of its weight on its shoulders, and lose its carriage as well as the purity of its gait.

Waldemar Seunig *Horsemanship*

However, since these links are so close, there is also the danger that incorrect attempts at collection may impair the very qualities needed to enhance it:

Premature or incompetent efforts towards collection reinforce inborn one-sidedness. The horse will evade the constraint by refusing to move the weaker hindleg in the direction of the centre of gravity.

Horses can be made even more crooked than normal as a result of incompetent riding, especially by premature demands for collection. Restricting hands, ineffective legs, a seat that impairs impulsion, wrongly timed Parades which only affect the mouth or the neck, and disregard of a horse's fitness for the stress of collected work will always induce the horse to avoid the painful effort by turning its quarters to one side...

Ulrik Schramm *The Undisciplined Horse*

The Collected Gaits

The extracts that follow have been listed under the headings walk, trot and canter for ease of reference. However, as will be evident from the extracts themselves (especially those relating to walk) this does not imply actual precedence in the training programme.

Collected Walk

John Winnett makes it clear that collected walk is not the province of the young, partially trained horse:

It is obvious that a young or untrained horse will not have the physical qualities needed to erect himself in self-carriage to perform a correct collected walk, the degree of engagement being entirely dependent upon the physical development of the horse.   John Winnett *Dressage as Art in Competition*

While Seunig comments:

Producing collection at the walk is no doubt one of the most difficult jobs a rider is called upon to do. We often see the so-called 'well-made' horses, even those that have won high prizes in dressage tests, committing more basic faults at the walk than at any other gait...   Waldemar Seunig *Horsemanship*

For this, *the most difficult exercise in riding,* even a talented horse under a superior rider will have to wait until approximately the end of the second year's training...

The collected walk should...be attempted...then only for short intervals...

The collected walk...and the extended walk...are definite proof, guarantee and end result of the entire previous training of the horse. This gait, with its high action carried by the flexed hocks,

Waldemar Seunig's own drawing of collected walk from
The Essence of Horsemanship.

its elegant and fluid cadence and its confident and easy contact, belongs in the realms of the High School...

Waldemar Seunig *The Essence of Horsemanship*

Müseler warns that riders should not deceive themselves with false impressions:

It is hardly possible to judge the collection of a horse by the carriage of his head and neck alone or by the lowering of his hind quarters. Collection can only be observed by watching him closely during action...At the walk a good horse should place his hind hoofs about eight inches ahead of the hoof-prints of his front feet...this is the normal action of an uncollected horse. With increased collection, that is, as soon as the action gets higher...the action becomes shorter and the hind legs are no longer placed in front of the fore legs. On the other hand, *this lagging behind of the hind legs is not yet* [i.e. of itself] *the proof of good collection.* Horses with a lazy action, 'bad movers', tired and overworked horses also leave their hind legs behind.

Wilhelm Müseler *Riding Logic*

Wynmalen also warns against the dangers of false impressions and explains why true collection in the walk is hard to obtain:

There is no pace at which it is easier to obtain a pretty-looking head carriage, giving the impression of collection, than the walk...There is no method either, by which it is easier to ruin the horse. The reader will recall...that no form of collection is of any value unless it is a result of lightening the forehand by increased activity of the quarters.

Now the walk is essentially a pace which is by nature unsuited for this purpose...in the walk...the horse has never less than two legs in support; in fact, support on two legs alternates with support on three. The distribution of weight varies constantly, from back to front and from side to side; there never is any concentration of balance, nor the degree of muscular tension, of energy and impulsion, whereby...carriage and lightness can be truly created.

Consequently attempts at achieving 'carriage' by the use of the walk alone will fail, because the pace does not lend itself to the creation of compressed energy. Instead, a semblance of results will be achieved by shortening the forehand, pulling the head into the body and not by driving the body up to the head. That, as we have seen...results in a closing of the shoulder, in the destruction of free forward movement, in a mouth behind instead of on the bridle and, more often than not, in destruction of the pure four-time gait. High-couraged horses may be induced to jog...or else the horse may tend to amble. The demanded increase of energy, which it is difficult for the horse to deliver at this gait, may induce him to approach the hoof-beats of each lateral pair of legs. Instead of absolutely regular intervals, 1-2-3-4...the horse may tend to...1.2–3.4.

He then gives an example of how work in the different gaits can be complementary:

Fortunately, all these difficulties can be avoided quite easily by allowing carriage, energy, rhythm and collection to develop at the trot and from the trot and, in conjunction with it, at the walk also...

Good head carriage can only be obtained naturally, without effort and without detriment, as the result of lightness through mobility of the quarters. That mobility is not a natural characteristic of the walk.

But it is of the trot. Especially the cadenced, highly energetic collected trot. And the whole of the horse's bearing at that trot, his grace, his lightness and his mobility are precisely the attributes we wish to preserve in the collected walk also.

So, it is plainly indicated that we should develop the collected walk, the really collected walk that is…light, expressive and graceful…from the collected trot.

Once we have progressed so far that the transitions from the collected trot to the collected walk have become fluent and light, it will be easy to maintain the horse's bearing, and his mobility, at the walk also…

Henry Wynmalen   *Dressage A Study of the Finer Points of Riding*

Henry Wynmalen riding collected walk on Ibrahim. From Dressage A Study of the Finer Points of Riding.

The beneficial effects of the trot upon the walk are also mentioned by Podhajsky and Brooke:

Only through systematic physical training in the trot and the maintenance of full impulsion will the collected walk drop like ripe fruit into the lap of the rider...The work at the collected walk will not be intensified until the end of the training.

Alois Podhajsky *The Complete Training of Horse and Rider*

Both the extended walk and even more the collected walk...will develop and improve as the horse comes to hand in extended and collected work at the trot.

Geoffrey Brooke *Horsemanship Dressage & Show-Jumping*

Describing the introduction of collected walk, Brooke recommends a patient approach, with the emphasis on retaining the forward impulse:

Lt. Col. A.L. d'Endrödy riding Clarion in collected walk from d'Endrödy's Give Your Horse a Chance.

Having taught your horse to move forward freely, his movements and carriage can by degrees be further controlled by the rider's legs and hand. The collected walk must not be allowed to relapse into a slovenly shuffle. Impetus must be maintained. By inducing more active anticipation by the hocks the weight is brought back with the head automatically raised and bent at the poll, the rider employing adequate leg pressure for this impulsion which he retains with light finger-tip tension on the reins...

Progressively the horse will learn to respond...At first we must only attempt a few strides at this collected pace, then change to the ordinary walk and later again attempt the collected walk. This will relieve the horse of undue strain and gradually he will appreciate what is required of him. A few collected paces executed correctly, followed by relaxing into an ordinary walk, will prevent the horse becoming upset and...instead of resisting he will start to respond and improve with each lesson.

Geoffrey Brooke *Horsemanship Dressage & Show-Jumping*

Initial straightness, precise co-ordination of the aids and patience are themes addressed by Wätjen:

In order to collect a horse at a walk it must walk absolutely straight...When the horse has learned to flex and has acquired a proper head position...and is light in the mouth, then the rider should drive it forward with both legs on a straight line. With braced back, and elbows at his sides, the rider should restrain with the reins, so that this restraint is transferred from the rider's wrists, elbows and lower part of the back, to the back of the horse. It must be strictly observed that the hand *restrains,* in the precise sense of the word, and does not pull back, so that the driving aid is greater than the restraining one. In this way the horse is *guided* into the proper head carriage from the rear to the front, and not *dragged* into it. The time spent riding at a collected walk remains entirely dependent on the horse's individual reaction. If the horse finds it difficult, the rider should be satisfied with a short period, repeating the exercise a little later, until the horse has learned to maintain the desired position...The rider must be particularly careful to see that the sequence of the paces is correct, and that collection is not achieved by upsetting the true, steady walk.   Richard Wätjen *Dressage Riding*

Belasik discusses the role of the rider's posture in the correct application of the aids. Like Wätjen, he emphasises the need for the change in outline to be produced correctly:

From the ordinary walk, which is a horse's natural walk on the bit, the rider collects the walk. In the collected walk, the rider is in as perfect a position as possible. The rider gently takes up more contact with the reins. The connection to the back and the seat is emphasized...The rider's hips subtly keep the horse from losing any power or slowing down the tempo while the step is shortened. The legs are ready to reinforce the seat aids if the horse stiffens even slightly in the mouth or the neck. The rider's back is poised and the center of gravity is directly over the legs. Because of this gathering up with no reduction of power, the step of the horse changes and its overall shape changes. The step becomes higher and might *seem* slower because of the higher arc in the suspension phase. The shape seems rounder, not *because* the overall length of frame has been reduced, but because of *how* it has been reduced. If it were reduced and the horse was hollow in the back, any compression would become grotesque, with the tail pointed up, and the cervical vertebrae strained upwards in a 'U' shape. However, when the horse is already on the bit and engaged in the ordinary walk, a compression of this round form is made even rounder, into a shape which more closely resembles a 'C'. The compression of the horse's power is palpable. An observer could easily imagine the horse stepping into a cadenced piaffe.   Paul Belasik *Dressage for the 21st Century*

Seunig describes the collected walk in the following terms:

The hindquarters are lowered in accordance with their increased engagement...The relieved forehand steps out higher, and the neck rises upward almost vertically from the withers...The driving action of the rider passes through the active back and the supple poll unhindered into the chewing mouth, where it is converted into correct head carriage by the gently supporting reins. The centre of gravity is displaced towards the rear, and all it now requires is a relatively pronounced engagement of the bent hind legs, so that their hoofprints alight behind the hoofprints of the forelegs...   Waldemar Seunig *Horsemanship*

However, he, too is concerned about the co-ordination of the aids and, especially, that this co-ordination may be compromised by overuse of the rider's hands:

All riders, except those possessing an enviable knowledge and ability, naturally tend to give the hands precedence when combining various controls. This is most serious in exercises at the walk. That is why the hands must be supervised with more rigorous self-discipline – to prevent them from interfering with the interplay of the horse's muscles – at the walk than at other gaits, where mistakes of control are partly balanced out by impulsion...
                                   Waldemar Seunig *Horsemanship*

Indeed, this is one of a series of faults and corrections he describes in *The Essence of Horsemanship*...

Fault: The rider exaggerates the restraining aids in an attempt to collect the horse…He allows, generally unknowingly, the reins to dominate, and operates from the front to the rear rather than…from the rear to the front. The result is hindquarters stiffening themselves against the pressure of the reins and the loss of a rhythmic, expressive cadence. *Correction:* The rider must watch his hands with strict self-discipline. They must never interfere with the movement of the horse and the bringing under of the hindquarters. Therefore a passive hand, which waits for the hindquarters brought and delivered to them by the rider's back.

…the others being:

Fault: The collected walk is insufficient because it is being asked of a horse which is not yet fully supple in his back or joints. Or, it *becomes insufficient* during a period of work because the horse has been ridden too long in collection and has not been given the opportunity to stretch from time to time and rest. *Correction:* Obvious in the description of the faults.

Fault: Over-eager horses try to free themselves from the rider's legs. *Correction:* The rider's legs remain quietly and gently on the horse: this is the best way to calm the horse. Soon the rider will feel a more relaxed and obvious four-beat measure against his legs…

Fault: Often because of restlessness strong, nervous horses will adopt short, hasty and impure strides…*Correction:* First of all, with a quiet clinging leg…calm the horse. When the even four beats have been re-established, preferably without half-halts, if at all possible…the driving leg of the rider can now gradually and gently be applied sufficiently to achieve a more lively gait, without attacking the horse which is only too ready to tense himself anew in response to kicking aids. As a result of being driven forward gently in a four beat stride the horse will now be induced to accept an even and soft contact with more confidence than before.

Fault: The rider exaggerates the alternating driving aids or drums the horse constantly and simultaneously with both legs. The simultaneous hammering...disturbs the rhythm of the gait...Besides, such driving aids only result in the stiffening of the hindquarters and back, which breaks up the harmony between the hindquarters and forehand and results in the horse starting to pace or jog.

Fault: The rider demands too soon...a lively rhythm of the sort which can only be maintained with a horse that is fully schooled, completely supple in his hocks and has a stately carriage. The beginner or young horse is not yet equal to this dual assignment...his strides become hasty and fragmented...or they can stiffen into a pacing-like sequence.

Waldemar Seunig   The Essence of Horsemanship

Further to this last fault, Seunig makes an interesting observation in *Horsemanship* that:

The notion that at the walk the timing must be the same for all rates, as it is at the trot and gallop, is largely responsible for the fact that some dressage horses walk with a hasty, broken and hurried step...

This general principle holds good for the collected walk of a well-trained horse, which walks smoothly with haunches that have been rendered completely supple. Following it blindly, however, may become dangerous if too much is demanded at the beginning of work at the collected walk. The horse would defend itself against the twofold requirement that it take lofty as well as very lively steps more successfully here than at the other gaits, in which impulsion and the briefer contact of the leg with the ground come to our assistance. It would take refuge in the hasty steps mentioned above, which often stiffen into a pace-like sequence.   Waldemar Seunig *Horsemanship*

Clearly, Seunig is making a specific point here that demanding too much precision in the early stages may, in some cases, prove counter-productive. However, purity of movement remains the long-term goal:

Once the horse has achieved the same lively timing in a pure four-beat walk as at the other types of walk, with its hindquarters lowered, all its joints loosened and flexed and its steps elevated, we have the manège walk.   Waldemar Seunig *Horsemanship*

Collected Trot

The characteristics of collected trot are described by Winnett...

In the collected trot, the horse reaches collection and cadence just short of the passage, gaining in height what he loses in length. The strides must maintain perfect rhythm, cadence, and engagement of the hocks. The engagement and flexion of the joints of the hind legs allow the haunches to lower, shifting more weight to the hindquarters, thus allowing the neck and head to raise. The poll must remain the highest point of the neck, and the head must be engaged slightly in front of the perpendicular. If the collection of the head is perpendicular, or behind it, the horse will lose impulsion.

John Winnett *Dressage as Art in Competition*

...Belasik:

The collected trot is developed from the working trot and becomes a trot in the same tempo. However, the collected trot covers less ground because the body travels in a shorter and higher trajectory. There is more flexion in the limbs of the collected trot than in the working trot – but then again, there is more flexion in the medium or extended trot than in the working trot. What is really different is that, in the collected trot, the rider restrains the forward urge by keeping the horse's feet more consistently under its mass. The result is that, when there is a complementary extension of the limbs, the force is more vertical. The flexing and extending rhythm of legs is not interrupted; it is adjusted. The rider is almost balancing the horse's body back so that the horse's legs can push the body up. Since the hind legs do the lion's share of the pushing, by definition, more weight will be placed on them. Of course, this is not accomplished by holding the horse back with excessive rein aids...If a rider pulls on the reins, the braking action will tip the mass forward just as your automobile tips forward when you apply the brakes.

Paul Belasik Dressage for the 21st Century

...and Wätjen:

With the *collected* trot the rider should not start too early...The horse should show elevated steps, not gaining much ground... and show proper rhythm with the maximum impulsion; in other words, this is the proper dressage position. The hindlegs should be well engaged, but the impulsion goes upwards, instead of forward...the horse becomes more compressed. Lively steps, proper cadence and suppleness are the criterion [sic] of a collected trot. Dragging and passage-like steps are signs of tension and unsystematic work.   Richard Wätjen *Dressage Riding*

It seems likely from the context that, in saying that the collected trot should not be started too early, Wätjen is referring to demands for the completed form. He goes on to say:

In developing the collected trot it is of great advantage to practise it for a short spell in the transition from the extended trot. The rider then makes use of the impulsion created by the extended trot. With half halts and simultaneous *driving aids* the horse becomes more collected...As with the extended trot, it takes some time before the horse can execute a true collected trot.

Richard Wätjen *Dressage Riding*

Richard Wätjen in collected trot, from Wätjen's Dressage Riding.

There is a consensus that the collected trot is developed from the early exercises based around the working trot – the length-ened strides providing, in embryonic fashion, the advantages Wätjen mentions in the context of the more advanced form. This early work is described by Podhajsky...

In order to make the young horse understand the collected trot better, the rider should use the *working trot,* which is between the ordinary trot and the collected trot, but this kind of trot should be regarded merely as a stepping stone. By frequent changes of speed the horse will acquire more activity in his steps. He will become accustomed to responding to the pressure of the rider's legs by immediately going forward and to decreasing the pace as

Collected trot of a horse under training at the Spanish Riding School, from Wilhelm Müseler's Riding Logic.

Major J. Handler on Conversano Benvenuta I at collected trot, from Waldemar Seunig's Horsemanship.

93

a result of the action of the reins supported by the back of the rider. Thus he should learn to concentrate on his rider and react immediately to the lightest of aids...the rider will reap the benefit of improvement in the contact, impulsion, obedience, and the action of the rein going through the body. This improvement will give him the opportunity to check the action especially when asking for collection...

Alois Podhajsky *The Complete Training of Horse and Rider*

...and Seunig:

Once our young horse has acquired the necessary suppleness of the hindquarters' joints as a result of full halts and backing, we begin to try to make the shortened trot that we have developed from the working trot more expressive and loftier. Frequent transitions from the middle trot to a shortened rate, and vice versa, will increase the springiness of the hindquarters. This alteration between stretching in a somewhat lengthened framework and bending in greater collection will increase the impulsion and carrying capacity of the hindquarters so much that *the shortened trot will turn into the collected trot...*

Waldemar Seunig *Horsemanship*

Seunig goes on to describe the further development of the collected trot...

The *development* of the collected trot is best achieved after a good medium trot has been executed, by gradually shortening the strides. At the same time it is important to retain lively yet cadenced steps flowing from a supple shoulder, and the impulsion achieved at the medium trot. The impulsion now is more elevated rather than forward. The engaged hindquarters to which the weight has shifted 'lifts' the forehand and makes possible its elegant, round movement...

Through the energy of impulsion mobilised from within himself, the horse is now prepared, in his physique and emotional attentiveness, to respond instantly to the slightest indications to change his tempo, posture, direction or gait.

Aids to the Collected Trot: With braced back and knees down, legs immediately behind the girth, the rider asks the horse to move his hind legs energetically. The sensitive hand keeps the mouth fresh. The poll appears to have been oiled to complete flexibility. The horse is straight!

...adding:

Just a few words more to characterize correct collection and how the rider will feel when it has been achieved. Thanks to the lithe play of the swinging back muscles...the rider will feel himself effortlessly drawn down into the saddle...The horse completely accepts the elasticity of the rider's back and legs...it is an easy task to lengthen...the strides...at will.

Waldemar Seunig *The Essence of Horsemanship*

Faults in the collected trot are summed up succinctly...

The main faults observed in the collected trot are irregular steps, which are the result of improper gymnastic training or lameness, and floating 'passage' steps, which are the result of too much tension, or lack of strength...

John Winnett *Dressage as Art in Competition*

Fault: Floating, *passage*-like strides. *Correction:* With less collection, drive forward. Energetic strides. Very gradually, with a light hand, try to shorten again. As soon as the rhythm slows, immediately drive forward and re-establish the oscillation of the back. Waldemar Seunig *The Essence of Horsemanship*

The rider must take care that in the collected trot the horse does not lose his impulsion and that the activity of the steps is maintained, a rhythmic and regular tempo kept. As the correctly executed collected trot is a considerable strain on the horse, it should be practised only for short periods and brought to an end before the horse shows signs of fatigue, otherwise the brilliancy of the steps will be lost.

Alois Podhajsky   *The Complete Training of Horse and Rider*

...and Seunig agrees with Podhajsky's sentiment to the extent of setting the same advice in italics:

The collected trot should be ridden only for short stretches and always alternated with freer gaits.   Waldemar Seunig   *Horsemanship*

Collected trot with trailing hindlegs; the horse is behind the bit and its neck is shortened. Ineffective seat and legs of the rider. This is not a properly collected trot.

Faulty movement in collected trot: Ulrik Schramm's own drawing from The Undisciplined Horse.

Collected Canter

The collected canter, in its correct form as described by Winnett, is a very elegant gait:

In the collected canter, the thorax rises in its sling to bring up the horse's back, weight is shifted to the rear, the haunches lower by virtue of increased flexion of the joints of the hind legs, the neck rises out of the shoulders in an elegant arc, the poll remains at the highest point, and the head is flexed almost to the perpendicular. The horse covers the ground in soft, energetic strides that maintain a perfect three-beat rhythm, engaging his hind legs just in front of the line of maximum lift. The horse must give the impression that he is ready to extend at the slightest suggestion.

John Winnett   *Dressage as Art in Competition*

However Steinbrecht warns that the collecting process should not be undertaken lightly:

The canter is a gait which very easily leads the inexperienced rider to incorrect shortening attempts. Not only is it a very widespread prejudice that a shortened canter is the touchstone of dressage training, the majority of horses also learn to escape correct work by incorrectly shortening their gaits. It can therefore not be repeated often enough…'Not *shortness* but *impulsion* characterizes a good collected canter.'

Gustav Steinbrecht   *The Gymnasium of the Horse*

Seunig echoes Steinbrecht's view on impulsion...

It is not simply the shortening of the stride that is characteristic of the collected canter, but the elastic spring of the hindquarters coming farther under which gives the rider the pleasant feeling that he is sitting in a well-sprung vehicle on a smooth highway.

Waldemar Seunig *The Essence of Horsemanship*

...and emphasises the point:

Let us repeat for the sake of emphasis that what matters in collecting the gallop is not shortening the steps as such. The chief underlying principle in this work...must be maintenance of vigorous freshness, liveliness, and cleanness of the stride...

Waldemar Seunig *Horsemanship*

Wynmalen explores the basic nature of canter, and elaborates on the pitfalls of incorrect attempts at collection...

The natural canter is a fairly slow gait, as compared with the gallop; it is also a...gait with a certain amount of natural collection; the horse carries his head and neck fairly high, places his hindlegs

Waldemar Seunig's own drawing of collected canter from
The Essence of Horsemanship.

well underneath his body and moves in an easy balance...

But, in dressage, we require the school-canter, which is very much slower and demands a much higher degree of collection to insure accuracy, ease and lightness of control. The horse's carriage, his bearing and the rhythm of his gait are much more defined than in the ordinary canter. He presents a more elegant and more impressive picture altogether.

Provided always that he has lost neither the pure three-time form of his canter, nor the comparative length of his stride, nor his impulsion. In fact, the slower the canter the greater the impulsion needs to be to preserve these qualities...

Riders all too frequently attempt to obtain a slow canter by pulling on the reins. Pulling on the reins implies the use of a backward action of the hands which is always...fatal. The effect of that action on the horse's mouth must destroy the freedom of his forward stride...It is quite possible to keep the horse cantering, notwithstanding that pull, by driving him on at the same time; certainly, but in what form?

...The front legs are prevented from reaching out, the hindlegs from treading under and the mouth ruined in the process; loins and back, instead of swinging more and more... become cramped and stiff, causing the rider to sit on top of that back instead of into it; the horse potters with his forelegs and is prevented from placing his hindlegs well under his body...

Henry Wynmalen *Dressage A Study of the Finer Points of Riding*

...his last point being summarised succinctly by Seunig:

Fault: The rider is trying to shorten the strides from medium canter to collected canter with the reins only. From the pre-dominance of the restraining aids, the horse drags its hindquarters and loses impulsion.

Waldemar Seunig *The Essence of Horsemanship*

There seems to be a diversity of opinion as to how the collected canter is best introduced. The danger of overusing the reins in trying to shorten the gait, with the attendant risks of loss of impulsion and crookedness, are certainly factors here. Podhajsky is one authority who talks of shortening the working gait, but he warns that it is important to do this discreetly and gradually, and emphasises the need to retain impulsion:

The time has now come to ask for the *collected canter*. The tempo must be shortened gradually by half-halts. In this exercise it is important to remember that the shortening must not be brought about by a slackening of the speed but by decreasing the length of the bounds. When teaching the collected canter, the rider has to be content at first with a lesser collection and the work must be for short periods, otherwise the activity of the hindquarters will be lost…The collected canter is even more difficult for the horse than the collected trot. The horse should become shorter throughout his whole body and the spring, as it were, should be more tightly compressed…Much impulsion is needed for this exercise.

Alois Podhajsky *The Complete Training of Horse and Rider*

He also makes use of the collecting effect of working on a circle (although this, presumably, presupposes that the horse is tracking true on the circle):

It may happen that young horses that are able to become more compressed (collected) when cantering on the large circle will become longer when taken on a straight line…The reason for this is that the rider can apply the pushing and holding aids more effectively on the large circle than on a straight line, and this is the secret of why the horse can be shaped more easily on the circle and why this work is of such great importance.

Alois Podhajsky *The Complete Training of Horse and Rider*

Seunig also makes use of the circle, although he disagrees with the idea of first introducing collection by shortening the working gait:

Aids: The rider, having prepared the horse…will now go into the canter on the circle, at first from the collected trot…with firm contact. It would be wrong, for the time being, to try to achieve a collected canter by shortening the more free cadence of the medium or working canter, as conversely, we have achieved, with the greatest of success, the shortened trot by shortening the active tempo of the medium trot…

Waldemar Seunig   The Essence of Horsemanship

Seunig also makes the point that the horse's suppleness is an important factor…

If the hindquarters engage pliantly, and the back is yielding and active, the rider will be carried along gently and evenly…If the hindquarters fly upward when the hind legs leave the ground… they are not yet fully loosened, but stiff in their principal joints… This fault cannot be corrected by increased seat control at the collected gait. The horse would defend itself against such attempted correction by increasing its stiffness and becoming crooked.

Smooth and gentle gallop departs for a short distance from a more positive *ordinary walk in hand,* followed by a halt after a few leaps before the haunches have had time to stiffen, will make the tendency towards this fault disappear, and the hindquarters will become more flexible. Stiffness of the haunches occurs very rapidly if the gallops are prolonged for too long a time…

…adding:

Once posture at the collected gallop has been further established by frequent gallop departs…from the walk, the transition may be

Major J. Handler on Conversano Benvenuta I at collected canter, from Waldemar Seunig's Horsemanship.

Collected canter: Miss J. Newberry on Pluto, from Wilhelm Müseler's Riding Logic.

made from the medium gallop to the collected gait.

Waldemar Seunig *Horsemanship*

Ulrik Schramm, who spent much of his time remedying faulty training, formed the opinion that:

It is always wrong to attempt to teach the horse to collect the canter by slowing the working canter. We must start the work of collecting the canter by frequently repeating transitions from the walk or the collected trot into canter, while paying great attention to the straightness of the horse's position prior to driving it forwards.   Ulrik Schramm *The Undisciplined Horse*

This view being shared by Steinbrecht:

The canter, particularly its collection, requires a much more complicated and careful development than the other gaits. Mistakes made here are very difficult to eradicate later, sometimes not at all.

At this opportunity reference should also be made quite generally to the significant difference between the first collecting work at the canter and that at the trot and walk. In the latter gaits the rider obtains the first collection by changing from a freer to a more restrained tempo, that is by using half-halts. In the canter, however, this collection must be obtained initially only by frequent transitions obtained with fine, light aids, first from a working trot, then from a walk, with the transition to the original gait also being executed with the same light, carefully measured aids.   Gustav Steinbrecht *The Gymnasium of the Horse*

The differences between canter and trot are also mentioned by Belasik, in an examination of how the aids are applied to collect the canter:

To collect the canter, the rider almost simultaneously begins to push the gait a little while closing the fingers and making the hand more passive. This dams up the power so that the trajectory of the stride begins to climb, covering less ground forward but becoming higher in its steps. As I have already made clear, this is not accomplished by increasing the leg aids but, if the rider pushes with the seat, when, and how much?

In the trot, which is more horizontal and more staccato in its rhythm than the canter, the driving seat might seem, paradoxically, a more steady or continuous means of pushing the horse, when needed, in these steady packets of energy. The

An incorrectly collected canter, showing resistance to the bit and a rigid back. But observe the stiffened shoulders of the rider, his rigidly braced back and his knee grip.

Incorrectly collected canter: Ulrik Schramm's own drawing from
The Undisciplined Horse.

canter, however, is different. There is really only one part of the stride during which the rider can push effectively...This is the moment in the stride when the hind legs are up off the ground and the horse's hips are going to swing under. If, at this point, the rider initiates more drive with the seat... the hind legs will come a little further under than they would without any encouragement. This further underside engagement of the horse is only possible if the topside (top line) stretches while the abdominals contract. If the rider were to drop down on the back of the horse at this moment and grind into the back muscles to try to drive the hind legs under, it would have exactly the opposite effect. Upsetting the stretch of the top line would directly affect the underside engagement. This is another example of how the principles of muscle movement... determine much of the training, whether laterally...or longitudinally...

To return to the mechanics of collecting the canter, the classical rider with a light seat but strong and flexible back pushes forward as the horse begins to rise in front of him. This forward push draws the rear end further under the belly. The rider's seat, crowding the pommel, does nothing to impede the horse's back muscles from stretching to allow the underside reach. Let me be quite clear on this. It does not mean that the rider stands up off the horse's back...like a jockey. This might get the rider maximum engagement, but in dressage, immediacy of response is necessary to extend then collect, collect then extend, etc. The seat must always be there, because it is the center of balance. As always during training, the legs reinforce the instructions of the seat. They do not do all the work themselves. They remind the horse to follow the rider's seat...

In the collected canter, the rider encourages more engagement of the hind legs with seat, back and legs and simultaneously restrains or contains this power with the reins – but must be very careful not to let the horse 'lie' in the reins. This will defeat collection and tip the horse onto the forehand. The mass of the horse is held, in a sense, over the hind legs so that the horse is taking a shorter stride, learning to carry the weight longer, flexing the hocks, stifles and hips more. If the rider pays a lot of attention to maintaining the same tempo, then the horse won't 'cheat' thereby making the stride shorter by just slowing down. Instead, it will make the stride shorter by collecting it, and the stride will keep its jump.

Paul Belasik Dressage for the 21st Century

The immediacy of response necessary to move smoothly between collection and extension, is also mentioned by Seunig:

The horse must show the ability, by fluid strides out of the engaged and flexed and increasingly weight-bearing hindquarters, to be ready at any moment to respond to the command to canter forward smoothly out of collection into long, free strides.

Waldemar Seunig The Essence of Horsemanship

While, in a picture of the ideal collected canter, Steinbrecht stresses the 'lively eagerness to go forward' which accompanies a stately progression:

If we paint the ideal picture of a canter that has been shortened correctly by way of collection, the spectator must gain the impression that the horse is imbued with the liveliest eagerness to go forward although it does not gain more ground than is possible for someone riding along at the walk. Such a canter is natural only by the spring-like activity of the three major joints of the hindquarters: the hip, the stifle, and the hock. This spring force must be developed to perfection...and the degree of its effect must be determined unconditionally by the rider's hands. The slightest pressure of the bit…must be sufficient to compress the springs...

It would be foolish to expect such a canter from every horse. Only the noble horse that is willing to go forward, whom nature has given a well conformed forehand, a back of medium length and, most importantly, strong, flexible and well-angled hindquarters will be able to perform it to perfection.

Gustav Steinbrecht *The Gymnasium of the Horse*

It seems clear that Steinbrecht's reference to the action of the bit 'compressing the springs' does not suggest that this collection is obtained simply by the action of the hand, but presupposes the existence of a high degree of impulsion and submission. Indeed, his picture of a stately, powerful canter under complete control represents the 'school' version of collected canter – which leads us to a brief consideration of the school gaits.

School Gaits

While space does not permit a detailed examination of the school gaits, we should certainly consider them out of respect, since they represent the ultimate refinements of collected work. Historically, most Masters have divided the training process into three phases. The first phase, often called the elementary or field school, represents the basic training of the young horse; the second phase, traditionally called the campaign school, represents the continuing development and enhancement of training, and the third phase relates to High School work. It is during the second phase that collection is developed – hopefully, with many horses, to a fairly advanced level. There is, however, a distinction between this level of collection and the ultimate collection of the exceptional horse trained in High School work. Podhajsky explains this by quoting H.E. von Holbein, author of the Spanish Riding School's *Directives,* published in 1898, the year in which von Holbein was appointed Director of the School:

The second phase of training is described by H.E. von Holbein as follows: 'Riding the horse in all paces, turns and figures in collection and full balance is the so called "Campaign School". Only when by this training suppleness, impulsion and skill have been obtained, accompanied by stamina, and when the intelligence has been developed, then, and only then can the rider proceed to art...'

    Alois Podhajsky   *The Complete Training of Horse and Rider*

The important point to note is that the distinction is, essentially, one of degree – the difference between considerable ability and virtuosity. There is no fundamentally different *principle* involved: work in the school gaits represents a continuum of what has gone before. It is true, however, that the school gaits can be considered the province of unusually talented horses trained by riders of exceptional ability.

    Here are some points made by the Masters on these issues:

School movements differ from balanced movements by their more elevated performance, by their greater impulsion, and by the decreased amount of ground covered at each stride. They require greater flexibility of the haunches, in other words collection, and thus a greater weight transfer to the hindquarters.

    Gustav Steinbrecht   *The Gymnasium of the Horse*

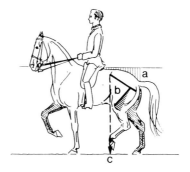

The School Walk
a = Lowering of the croup
b = Flexion of haunches
c = Plumb line from the hip joint

The School Trot
a = Lowering of the croup
b = Flexion of haunches
c = Plumb line from hip joint

The School Canter
a = Lowering of the croup
b = Flexion of haunches
c = Plumb line from hip joint

The school gaits, from Alfred Knopfhart's Dressage A Guidebook for the Road to Success.

A dressage horse must be seen to want to go forward; elevation, for him is of secondary importance...But for the High-School horse, elevation is the most important thing...the propulsive force of the tremendously powerful hindquarters must be contained, to be delivered in a predominantly upward direction; there must also be impulsion but its effect is at a different angle with the horizontal. Üdo Burger *The Way to Perfect Horsemanship*

The...secondary school is both an elaboration of what the horse learned in the previous school and an organic evolution from the simpler to the more difficult, constituting the transition to the lessons of the *haute école*...

The principal requirement for all these demands is a capacity for collection and a development of impulsion that is far above the average. The preceding training must have clearly told the rider whether this capacity for collection has reached its natural limits, fixed either by the horse's conformation or its disposition.

One thing is certain: among many thousands of horses, only a few will qualify for the university of higher dressage science...

There still are riding authorities who prefer to make a sharp distinction between the training of the general utility horse and that given in the *haute école*. They say that the manège horse that is brought to the highest expression of its flexibility and carrying capacity does not have to pass through the same initial stages of gymnastic training as any other saddle horse...

In reality, if we presuppose ideal training conditions, it is only the fully trained general utility horse that is able to become a manège horse, provided its spirit, machinery of locomotion, conformation, and industriousness qualify it for the high degrees of impulsion, responsiveness, and collection that are prerequisites for the *haute école*.   Waldemar Seunig *Horsemanship*

It is essential that the horse…should possess a good foundation before starting with a higher school collection. All the principles of training mentioned in the elementary dressage must be adhered to in the *Haute École*…

The perfect collection can only be gradually achieved as, by excessive and too early collection, the free forward movement would suffer and the horse would resist by going sideways and stiffening its back. The rider's hand must be absolutely still and steady with a supple wrist, as a restless hand in no way furthers the collection. On the contrary, the unsteady contact irritates the horse and it ceases to be sensitive to the proper rein aids…

A definite time at which to start with school collection…cannot be fixed. Feeling and experience will teach the rider how quickly he can progress in advanced training without overdoing it…

School collection is achieved by a higher degree of elevation and a simultaneous increased cadence.

The condition for this higher collection is based on the development of the hindquarters and the increased engagement of the hocks…This higher collection, connected with a correct elevation, leads with increased activity of the hindlegs to a gradual transference of the centre of gravity to the rear, and teaches the horse to use his hocks more flexibly in carrying the weight of the rider. By systematic training the horse learns to move in absolute self-carriage with elastic, supple hindquarters. The achievement of perfect collection is then only a matter of time, for this is the final aim…

         Richard Wätjen *Dressage Riding*

Principles of Lengthening

It seems fair to say that lengthening, in principle, is easier to define than collection. In lengthening, the horse increases his stride beyond its 'normal' length (which may be more or less defined by the working[1] gait), whilst retaining balance and tempo. However, as we have noted, there is a close correlation between collecting and lengthening – and this includes the common need for power and energy in the hind limbs. Although collecting and lengthening employ these qualities to different effect, the fundamental point is that they have to be available. The corollary to this is that, as with collecting, the horse's ability to lengthen co rectly will increase in accordance with correct physical development – another example of the need for progressive training.

The training in extension then has to proceed just as gradually as the training in collection. Only, in a sense, it is even more difficult, because it is so easy to drive the horse beyond his rhythm. And an extended trot without rhythm degenerates just as easily into a valueless 'run' as an indifferent collected trot may go to waste in an equally valueless 'jog'.

Henry Wynmalen *Dressage A Study of the Finer Points of Riding*

Initial work on lengthening is described by Winnett:

[1] 1 Medium, in walk.

112

Lengthening of the stride...is asked for in the beginning of training before the horse has gained sufficient suppleness and strength to perform the extended trot. In lengthening the stride, the horse extends his frame...reaches down with light flexion in his poll and 'chases' his bit forward: with his muscles lengthened, his back up and relaxed, the horse will cover as much ground per stride and show as much elasticity and suspension as his natural strength and cadence allow.

However, it is evident that this is primarily an exercise based around the working gait:

The lengthening of stride in the trot is the first longitudinal exercise. The transitions should be asked for out of the working trot and back into the working trot, because the horse has too much weight on his forehand to be able to move himself back into a collected gait at this stage of training.

Winnett does not, in fact, address the medium and extended work until quite an advanced stage in his training regime, stating of medium and extended trot:

These are developed out of high collection, total development of the musculature system, mechanical impulsion, and...self-carriage... If asked for too soon, the trot in general can be ruined...

John Winnett *Dressage as Art in Competition*

Although Seunig may have been prepared to begin this work at a somewhat earlier stage, this was clearly conditional upon the horse's physical development, and the introduction was to be gradual:

If after about nine months of training, the young horse's croup, back and stomach muscles have become strengthened, and the impulsion of the hindquarters and their capacity for flexing developed by the bending exercises are assured, the medium trot can be practised for short periods...

Waldemar Seunig *The Essence of Horsemanship*

This criterion of appropriate progression is repeated frequently as the Masters discuss the topic of lengthening.

Another key issue is the relationship between rein contact and the horse's balance. In pondering the initial thinking behind the inclusion of extended gaits in dressage tests, van Schaik moves on to this issue...

It is my opinion that the F.E.I. was stimulated by Caprilli to ask for extending movements in the dressage tests in order to get the riders out of the habit of pulling their horses together. I think that a misconceived interpretation of Caprilli is at the root of bad extensions. Caprilli wanted the horse unconstrained in going cross-country, so that the neck and back could be used. Unconstrained does not mean that the horse should go without any contact with the rider's hand, resulting in a disconnected horse. It does mean that the rider has an elastic contact with always straight reins 'never' loops and with the tension varying from featherlight to firm. The horse does not object to a firm contact as long as it is elastic; the horse often fights a dead hand, or one that is set or pulling. With this elastic contact, the rider is able to keep the horse in balance.

When either a lengthening of the stride or an extension is asked for in dressage competitions, one sees only too frequently that the rider lets go, losing all contact. The result is that the horse falls apart and loses his balance, because the hindlegs do not push any more and they spread far apart. To some it may give the impression of a lengthened fame, but it is a functionally incorrect lengthening, because the hindlegs do not push, the back is not engaged; as a result the horse loses his balance resulting in rushing or coming on the forehand...A far more serious mistake is to allow the horse to throw his front legs in the air and let them not only touch the ground later than the diagonal hindleg, but also bring the front feet back. In other words, the front foot is not touching the ground on the spot at which the foot in its highest elevation, pointed. This is a difficult mistake to correct...This movement is the result of a stiff back in the horse, and that is where the correction should begin...

It is a misconception that in the extended trot the horse should put his nose forward...In this connection it is interesting that Feverot de Kerbrech wrote that the head should be close to perpendicular...This misconception that the nose should be allowed to come forward may well be the reason that so many horses lose their balance or 'fall in two pieces', which is worse. According to Egon von Neindorff...the horse loses the maximum forward drive of the hindlegs if the rider allows the nose to come forward. And this maximum forward drive is what the rules ask for.

Dr. H.L.M. van Schaik *Misconceptions and Simple Truths in Dressage*

This issue is also addressed by Wynmalen:

It follows from the extended form itself that the horse must transfer more weight from his quarters on to his forehand. Consequently the contact he will take, must, of necessity, be more positive, even though it need never be heavy. So long as the horse urges forward there may be distinct contact, but not weight. Weight will only be felt if the horse urges downward as well as forward. Which, if it occurs, is a certain sign that the rider has either given insufficient rein or else...that the rider himself is pulling, even though he may not realize it.

But, without positive contact, the rider would not be able to regulate the increase of forward impulsion, which may be very great, into evenly regulated, absolutely equal strides...

Henry Wynmalen *Dressage A Study of the Finer Points of Riding*

Another consideration of lengthening the stride is the increase in speed that necessarily results. In discussing the lengthened forms of trot, Belasik deals unequivocally with this issue:

On the other side of the working trot from the collected form are the medium and extended trots. One of the first things that comes into play in the development of the longer trots is speed. If the trots are all to remain at the same tempo regardless of whether the horse lengthens or shortens, then it must be understood that speed will be a by-product of lengthening. If the horse takes twenty collected strides and twenty extended strides at the same tempo, it will cover much more ground in the twenty extended strides than in the twenty collected strides, in the same amount of time. Covering more ground in the same time means it is moving faster. Thus, when introducing the medium trot, the rider must know that it isn't the raw speed of travel that is to be kept the same as the working gait; it is the tempo. In other words, the rider cannot, and should not, stop the horse from speeding up when it lengthens, but the rider must watch that the tempo does not increase.   Paul Belasik *Dressage for the 21st Century*

It is clear that retaining proper control is a key factor when riding the lengthened gaits. Oliveira typifies the Masters' attitude in proscribing force in all situations. However, he also makes the telling point that, in the extended gaits, attempts to control the horse by force will backfire on the rider in no uncertain terms:

There are riders who sacrifice lightness, suppleness and gentleness by not hesitating to use force in order to maintain the horse at all costs in a fixed position. But they will only impose this forced position on the horse in reduced gaits. The horse takes control over the rider's force in extended gaits.

Nuno Oliveira *Reflections on Equestrian Art*

Lengthening the Gaits

As with the collected gaits, the extracts in this section are grouped under walk, trot and canter for ease of reference. Again, this does not necessarily imply a precedence in training.

Lengthening the Walk

Many authorities agree that the biomechanical nature of walk makes it the easiest gait to spoil, and there is a consensus that its variants should be approached only in due season, and even then with due care. Seunig explains the antecedents of extended walk, which provide the rationale for his timescale:

...the *extended walk* evolves out of the...preceding stages of the free walk...and out of the increased ability of the hindquarters to engage, developed from exercise at the collected walk, which also must result in increased ability to extend.

Waldemar Seunig *Horsemanship*

Just as the collected walk, the extended trot and...canter are the result of the whole previous schooling and gymnastic...education, so is the extended walk...As the perfection of the three walks the extended walk can only be the result at least after two years education of complete control.

Waldemar Seunig *The Essence of Horsemanship*

One of the criteria of a correct extended walk is that the strides become the longest of which the individual horse is realistically capable...

In the extended walk the lengthening process reaches its physical limit. For every horse, it is different. It does not matter how big the walk actually is. It matters only that each horse and rider reaches it.   Paul Belasik *Dressage for the 21st Century*

...without compromising his rhythm or stride pattern:

The long steps from the haunches...must be limited only by the horse's conformation and the regularity and purity of its steps, the hind feet alighting far ahead of the tracks of the forefeet. The horse must seek contact with the bit in free, natural carriage, its neck stretched forward and its nose seeking the hand, so to speak.   Waldemar Seunig *Horsemanship*

In this work the horse lengthens his stride to the greatest extent of his capabilities without hurrying his step. Success in this movement is not possible until the horse has formed a perfect mouth...If we attempt to develop the...extended walk before the horse's mouth is ready, we shall only succeed in hurrying his stride but not in lengthening it...

Henry Wynmalen *Dressage A Study of the Finer Points of Riding*

Wynmalen often made reference to the horse's 'mouth', not because he was obsessed with the 'front end', but because he understood that true lightness in hand was an indicator of balance and submission. The importance of retaining correct balance is stressed by Belasik:

The challenge of the extended walk is to maintain balance and tempo while the frame of the horse opens up. The reins offer a space for the horse to fill up. The neck must remain up, reaching out, not down; otherwise, the extended walk would turn into a kind of walk on a free rein. The balance would fall too far onto the forelegs and the hind legs would push the weight rather than carrying it.   Paul Belasik *Dressage for the 21st Century*

While Winnett points out that, in addition to affecting balance and rhythm, over-riding the horse may consequentially lead to a *shortening* of the strides:

The more the horse is urged forward in...lengthening, the more the diagonal support tends to become a lateral support, the lower the footfalls to the ground and, when pushed to the extreme, the walk will become completely lateral, or a two-beat amble...The rider must always be careful not to override these gaits for fear of disrupting the diagonal base of support and shortening the strides.   John Winnett *Dressage as Art in Competition*

This view is shared by Geoffrey Brooke...

Too often attempts at the extended walk result in a hasty shuffle with short quick strides.

Geoffrey Brooke *Horsemanship Dressage & Show-Jumping*

...and Seunig, who repeats the need for thorough preparation:

This type of...walk...is by no means the result of letting the horse move rapidly; rather it requires thorough preparation and training. A hasty step is far from an active step or a long one. The latter must come from the hindquarters and will act correctly only when the back, neck, and cervical vertebrae are loosened by equestrian action.

This means that the extended walk is the result and fruit of previous engagement of the haunches, from which it must be 'ridden out' in the truest sense of the word. *It can never be achieved by eternally toying with the surrendered reins.*

If the eagerness and action of the steps...turn into precipitate hurrying, if the tail does not swing *evenly* to both sides...or if the horse in passing to the extended walk chews on the yielding bit tossing its head or produces jarring shocks downward...we know that the preceding work was done under constraint and was therefore defective...   Waldemar Seunig *Horsemanship*

In his later book, *The Essence of Horsemanship*, Seunig reprises his view of what can be learnt from the transition into extended walk and the gait itself, and gives notes on errors and corrections:

The deportment of the horse in the transition to the extended walk will give a clear picture whether the previous work during collection has been achieved without forcing...Furthermore, a demonstration of the long extended walk is the proof that the horse in spite of its utmost stretching and utmost reaching has maintained control of his body and has maintained balance without having to rush.

Error: During the transition to the extended walk, the horse pulls the rein with stiffened poll and tossing head out of the rider's hand, instead of seeking the hand with feeling lips and...stretching of the neck naturally. *Correction:* The previous work at collection has been forced. The back never gave in. Joints and muscles are not loose. The horse revenges itself as soon as it feels a freeing of the reins...commence by...relaxing the horse, then achieve proper collection; and only after this...again ask for extended walk.

Error: The briskness of the hitherto ground-covering strides becomes hasty. The steps are short and hasty. The tail, instead of swinging in cadence with the gait, becomes stiff... *Correction:* Softer leg aids, not abrupt.

Waldemar Seunig *The Essence of Horsemanship*

This last error and correction refer us back to the problem of over-riding the extended walk. The matter of softer leg aids is addressed by the highly practical Brooke, who recommends taking advantage of the horse's natural instincts, rather than strong aids, to produce extra activity. (His need to explain alternate leg aids may be rooted in the fact that, as a former cavalry instructor, he perhaps taught inexperienced riders, whose instinct was to use both legs together.)

A horse must be made to walk out boldly, keeping on a straight line and gradually working up to the extended walk...To make the horse walk out, the rider's legs should not be applied simultaneously...but alternately...Advantage can be taken of the horse's natural inclination to stride out when he knows he is turned towards his paddock or his stables. At the walk for home and dinner he will show eagerness to extend his paces and can be encouraged as just explained, while periodically checking him slightly for a dozen strides or so. Then again you indicate that you want him to walk out (which he is only too eager to do) with your leg applied...as before. By this simple ruse you are achieving much more than you would in a riding school.

Geoffrey Brooke *Horsemanship Dressage & Show-Jumping*

As we shall see in a moment, Brooke was not alone in recognising the value of working in the open when introducing lengthened strides.

Extended walk, from Geoffrey Brooke's Horsemanship, Dressage & Show-Jumping.

Lengthening the Trot

It is noteworthy how many of the great Masters, whose natural home we so readily imagine to be the manège, were in fact staunch advocates of working in the open, when they considered this to be expedient. The following extract is part of a passage in which Decarpentry describes the benefits, not only of working in the open, but on differing terrain and going. It is noteworthy that he uses the horse's natural instincts not only to obtain maximum forward movement in response to minimal aids, but also to retain the *desire* to move forward, so essential to the performance of good downward transitions.

The...task of the trainer will be to advance the gymnastic training of his pupil...to...maximum lengthening of the trot on straight lines; to develop the horse's sensitivity to the aids so that, on their indications, the variations of speed for which his mechanism has been prepared, can be executed with exactness.

This work must be practised out of doors, on good straight roads. In the manège, its results would be practically nil, and would remain negligible even in a very large outdoor school because of the insufficient length of the straight lines and the constant and marked changes of direction imposed upon the horse. While he is developing the training, the trainer must endeavour to use the horse's instinct to best advantage and, at least in the beginning, to act always in conformity with the horse's natural impulses. Subsequently, he will still avoid opposing these as much as possible, until the horse's increased sensitivity to his aids gives him the certainty of being capable of counteracting any natural, instinctive manifestations.

Thus, the first changes of speed[1] will be demanded on the way back to the stable.

Lengthenings will then be executed 'generously' in response to a minimum leg activity and, when slowing down, the horse's desire for a greater speed will still exist, as this constitutes the spirit of academic work and the key to its brilliancy.

General Decarpentry *Academic Equitation*

---

[1] As noted earlier (see Belasik quotation in Principles of Lengthening), it is perfectly legitimate to use the term 'speed' in this context, provided that it relates to changes in stride length, rather than stride frequency.

Wynmalen was another great advocate of working outdoors:

The school is not an ideal place for the practice of extended paces. The straight lines are much too short, and the many turns and corners make it impossible for the horse to persevere for any length of time in the right type of action with the hindlegs.

Henry Wynmalen *Dressage A Study of the Finer Points of Riding*

Within the confines of the school, the diagonal represents the longest straight line. However, Belasik offers an interesting rationale for introducing lengthened work down the long sides:

The lengthened trots are best introduced along the wall. The clean line of direction will help to keep the horse straight when lengthening. If the horse holds too much residual crookedness and the stride lengthens it will become uneven and, if more power is added or the shape is lengthened further, the horse will naturally break into canter. A second, associated, problem is that if the horse is not straight and the rider lengthens the stride across the diagonal, the crooked horse will drift in the free space. Then, when the rider tries to push the drifting horse back on line, the rider's strong leg aid again gets perceived as a canter aid, and the horse breaks gait or loses power because he is fighting the correction from the leg. This actually ends in a shortening, or quickening, of the stride. Both problems are corrected by the rider making sure that the horse is very even and straight before opening up the frame.

Paul Belasik *Dressage for the 21st Century*

The biomechanics of these lengthened trots are described by Winnett:

In the medium and extended trots, the horse lowers his haunches by flexion of the joints of his hind legs, and transfers weight

John Winnett riding medium and extended trot, from Dressage as Art in Competition.

125

and the centre of gravity to the rear. This allows the forehand to rise, and the forelegs to move forward in even, rounded strides…The hind legs must reach to a point just short of the line of maximum thrust. The fore and hind legs must compose an outline of two compasses opened to the same degree. The only difference between the medium and extended trots is that in the extended trot there is an increased flexion and thrust of the hindquarters resulting in greater elevation, impulsion and self-carriage.   John Winnett *Dressage as Art in Competition*

While the aids and their effects are discussed by Wätjen:

By engaging the hindlegs with increased driving aids, the rider induces the horse to use his forelegs freely from the shoulders. The artificial cramped stretching of the forelegs, whereby the strides do not gain sufficient ground is wrong and unnatural. The hindlegs must follow the diagonal without stepping sideways or moving too much apart. The increased driving aids, together with the restraining influence of the hands, teach the horse to increase the pace with an elastic back and a supple head and neck position...

At the beginning the rider should not use too strong driving aids, as this results in uneven paces of the hindlegs and the horse leaning on the bit. With these movements the rider should not hurry, but only gradually demand the full development of the extended trot.   Richard Wätjen *Dressage Riding*

Seunig makes specific reference to the qualities of medium trot, and how these are attained:

The medium trot is not a working gait, but as a schooling gait and an aid to the gymnastic development it is essential…[Its purpose is] the improvement of the gait by means of extending thrust and impulsion. Stabilizing the balance, carriage and posture of the horse by means of greater engagement of the hindquarters with resulting flexion of the neck and poll. Confident obedience to the aids...

The characteristic feature of the medium trot is the lengthening and energetic action of the strides. Since this is achieved through the rider's balance and through the flexion of the hocks, the forehand is enabled to lift and extend the forelegs with complete freedom. The forefeet touch the ground at the spot where the toes point to at the moment of highest elevation. The action of the forehand must, with the utmost of precision and expressiveness remain round and even. Cramped and choppy stretching of the forelegs indicate false tension...

The rider drives the horse by gradually increasing leg aids...into a stronger, more balanced movement...The strides should become longer and more expressive, however the rhythm should remain the same...

The horse extends on the bit, with the nose slightly ahead of the vertical in a beautiful carriage; and allows the impulsion to flow from the rear to the front through the poll. This impulsion is regulated by the rider's hand supported by the action of his lower back and is transmitted as needed to the horse's joints to serve as a spring or to the bracing weight of the hindquarters. The elastic impulsion of the hindlegs forward and upward is primarily and initially a result of their flexion and engagement and occurs *before the full extension* of the joints...

With the horse's greater acceptance of the bit, the bend of the poll becomes assured. The hindquarters having become lowered in the development of impulsion a higher head and neck carriage results – a relative elevation. The bend at the poll must be maintained; without that, the medium trot will inhibit any advancement and will also damage the joints...

He goes on to stress that:

To begin with, this exercise should be done only for the briefest of periods...For horses with a weak back, the rider should commence at first with rising trot.

Waldemar Seunig *The Essence of Horsemanship*

This use of rising trot in certain circumstances is expanded upon by Belasik:

To begin with, a rider who has natural gifts, or has practiced well, can remain sitting in the trot, which should afford the best control. However, if the horse is naturally a little short-striding or tight in the back, it is probably better to use the rising trot, so the horse will have no excuse not to free up the back a little for the longer reach. Paul Belasik *Dressage for the 21st Century*

'Fluid long-striding middle trot': Col. M. Thommen on Directeur. From Waldemar Seunig's Horsemanship.

Seunig also addresses various errors in the medium trot and offers corrections. These include:

Error: The horse bores on the bit. The hind legs push too hard and the whole weight is pushed onto the forehand. *Correction:* Frequent transitions between the medium trot and the working trot. The necessary half-halts will cause the horse to yield more…so that the hindquarters are obliged to carry more of the weight.

Error: The horse hurries when asked to lengthen…becomes irregular and carries his head and neck too high, without using his back. *Correction:* Calmly return to the working trot! Increase it only after the long, rhythmic strides have been re-established and…the horse accepts the hand and resumes oscillation of the back.

Error: The forelegs stretch in a stiff and jerky motion. The fore feet touch the ground behind the spot at which the toes pointed at the moment of highest elevation. [Seunig adds: In spite, or maybe because of this, the gallery will applaud!] *Correction:* Decrease the tension on the rein.

Error: The gait becomes passage-like, floating, with a taut, unyielding back. Admiring reaction from those on the ground! *Correction:* Through energetic working trot with an oscillating back, re-establish the liveliness of the gait.

Waldemar Seunig The Essence of Horsemanship

Schramm points out that certain errors appearing in medium trot may be attributable to insufficient development of the back muscles:

It is when the speed of the trot has to be increased to a medium trot that the gait will be seen to become disconnected if the horse has not been properly trained to use its back muscles. It hurries instead of lengthening its strides; it can be observed...to go wide behind, with stiffened hocks, and to show the soles of its hooves. Alternatively, it may forge when urged on, because its hindfoot is coming down before its forefoot is out of the way.

Ulrik Schramm *The Undisciplined Horse*

While Decarpentry highlights an evasion that may become evident when developing the longer strides:

Waldemar Seunig's own drawings of medium trot from The Essence of Horsemanship. *The picture above shows correct movement, the picture right (with Seunig's own caption) shows faulty movement.*

The main difficulty in the work of developing the trot is the horse's propensity to break into the canter when asked to increase his speed, and this propensity can turn into a resistance if one does not take care.

In the first place one should avoid breaking into the canter due to abruptness when demanding increased speed, or to lack of firmness or suppleness of the seat, or in general to any asymmetries in the rider's position, movement or aids.

The so-called medium trot of a 'stiff-legged mover'. The hind legs strike off too far back and push the weight onto the forehand. When the horse moves off, the shoes of the hind feet are visible too much and for too long. The hocks swing to the rear and upward in the direction of the tip of the tail, instead of *forward* and upward. The horse resembles a swimming duck, whose webbed feet pushing to the rear are used for propulsion only, the weight being carried by the water.

The horse's depressed back is not moving elastically but is held down rigidly. Its deepest point – a 'hollow' – is just slightly behind the withers. The rider is unable to sit down to the contracted back and is thoroughly tossed about; the rider 'looks down' and rides holding his hands as if he were playing the piano.

If the horse does break into a canter, he must be stopped without brutality, but quickly and firmly so that he can associate this sort of reprimand with its object, i.e. breaking into canter. Without raising his voice, the rider will thereupon utter the command: 'trot', and will repeat this procedure every time the horse commits the same fault.

This serious fault often requires much time to correct, but correction must be tenaciously persevered with, until it is completely achieved.   General Decarpentry *Academic Equitation*

The benefits of a good medium trot are summed up by Belasik...

A good medium trot will show that the rider has control of the lengthening process. It is also useful for practicing the accordion-like back exercises. If the extended trot were used to lengthen the stride in everyday practice, the extreme effort would be too demanding for more continuous training repetitions.

...who goes on to elaborate on the extended form:

The extended trot is the ultimate length of trot available to a given horse. Obviously, different horses will have different sizes of extended trot. The extended trot should show nearly equal activity of the hind and forelegs. The cannon bones should be approximately parallel when in full extension. If the fore cannon is angled at 45 degrees to the ground, the opposite hind cannon should show a similar angle. Extended trots that show dramatic reach with the foreleg, but an unmatched hind leg with half the reach, have to be considered faulty. Too much disparity will demand that the horse hollow its back as in the Spanish walk, which is not the aim of the powerful, gymnastic, extended trot. When executed correctly, the extended trot shows the maximum of swing, elasticity and strength. It should never appear restrained, tight or false in any way. When it is coupled with smooth, collecting transitions, it can be a proof of mastering the forces of impulsion. Furthermore, when this is done with light reins, it approaches art.

Paul Belasik *Dressage for the 21st Century*

Wätjen echoes Belasik's stricture that the extended trot should not be executed too often, and adds further comments on its form:

Not until the horse has learned to move correctly at the extended and collected trot, with proper smooth transitions, can one start to obtain the maximum extension...This maximum extension should not be practised to often, and should only be regarded as the result of correct training...

At this maximum extension...the utmost engagement of the hocks and the greatest impulsion are imperative and so is a proper lengthening of the neck. Under no condition should a...shortening of the neck be apparent. The rider should be able to drive his horse forward with a light contact, but with increased impulsion, gaining maximum ground in self carriage...Self carriage and balance are the two important factors.

The extended trot is always the result of methodical training on sound principles. Smooth transitions provide one of the best proofs of a well trained horse...

Richard Wätjen *Dressage Riding*

In highlighting the need for great impulsion, Oliveira points to the connection between collection and extension and describes an ideal extension flowing out of true collection:

The extended trot can only be obtained through extreme impulsion. For this to be true, it must be executed from the peak of collection in the school trot. It must be ample, and must not include any harshness or precipitation in the gait.

Even at the maximum extension of the trot, the horse must keep his legs supple. The movement must not be rough. The so-called extended trot, in which the horse stiffens his back, gesticulating with his lower front legs as if 'shooting the cuffs', pulling on the reins below a rider who uses his legs at every stride cannot be considered as being in the domain of impulsive, classical equitation.

The true extended trot is the one which is the result of maximum impulsion in collection.

The Spanish stallion, Excelso, in extended trot, showing the old rule of thumb that, in extension, the fore and hind cannon bones should be approximately parallel. From Paul Belasik's Dressage for the 21st Century.

During the last strides of cadenced trot, passage, or piaffer, the rider, by opening his fingers, allows the horse to extend.

The animal needs no pushing, his back stays flexible, his hind legs well engaged under him and detaching themselves from the ground, his fore legs sent well ahead, as their movement leaves the shoulder and goes right to the front of his shoe.

The horse should not throw out his legs towards the ground, but rather stretch them forward, as if he were trying to reach the farthest distance possible with his feet.

Nuno Oliveira *Reflections on Equestrian Art*

A phase of extended trot not often depicted – the horse about to unleash the power of the hind limb – from Paul Belasik's Dressage for the 21st Century.

In *Horsemanship*, Seunig writes:

The *extended trot*, like the middle trot, is a gait that serves gymnastic training of the horse. It is also a touchstone that shows us how much impulsion and poise we have managed to develop in the horse...

The horse should not be called upon for the extended trot before the end of the second year of training or even later, for this gait, with its very long strides originating from lowered hindquarters, is the end result...of well-planned gymnastics, making extraordinarily high demands upon thrust, impulsion, and equestrian poise.   Waldemar Seunig *Horsemanship*

He develops his theme in *The Essence of Horsemanship*...

While the collected trot improves the carriage and posture of the horse which is moving with impulsion, elegantly and fluidly – but not with a long reach – the purpose of the extended trot, is an intensification of the medium trot, from which it is developed, especially in increasing the engagement, and energetic action of the hind legs...

It develops…the thrust of impulsion to the degree where it is limited only by the horse's conformation and temperament. It serves as a test and mirror for the degree to which we have been successful in developing the impulsion, the driving force and the carriage of the horse...

The extended trot must only be the natural succession of the maximum impulsion and derive from the hocks. Thereby the extended trot is the proof of the degree of our success in improving the carriage and impulsion of the horse.

...and goes on to say of the rider:

The more free the tempo is, the more the rider must go along with the motion, controlling the horse with his lower back and seat. Despite less collection, the horse must be supple in the poll and always be ready to champ the bit.

During the correct extended trot, the rider remains easily and without effort in the saddle. The oscillating, shock-absorbing back draws him close from back to front in the movement and at the same time into the saddle. The rider has the feeling of *riding uphill* and no difficulty in sitting to the powerful, yet even and elastic, oscillating movements of the back which keep him deep in the saddle.

If the preparation has been too hasty and the back is not pliant enough, then we must – which would profane a classic performance…resort to a rising trot. Therefore a rider should aim to show his horse in the extended trot by sitting deeply and easily…so as to prove the preparation for this movement has been correct.   Waldemar Seunig *The Essence of Horsemanship*

Seunig's remarks on the rider's seat are pretty much a reprise of his comments in *Horsemanship*:

As for the rider, we might add that 'as he has made his bed, so will he sleep in it' at the extended trot. If he has managed to keep the back active, that is, pulsations elastic, during the entire course of dressage, he will find no difficulty in sitting out the powerful but regular and springy pulsations of the back in a correctly developed extended trot.

But if training was hastened too much, and the back has not become pliant, the posting trot must be resorted to for expediency. That is why every rider presenting his horse stays in the saddle in an effort to prove that his preparatory work was correct.

This should not be taken, however, as criticism of the posting trot as such; it is an indispensable aid to training.

Waldemar Seunig *Horsemanship*

Capt. Frank on Cyprian at extended trot, from Waldemar Seunig's Horsemanship.

Seunig's comments on the rider's seat no doubt reflect the consensus view, but an interesting slant on the subject is provided by Wynmalen:

In general, the high-couraged horse delivers his extension generously, without needing any great amount of drive from his rider; with such horses there is no need to use any other than the rising trot. But there are other, more cold-tempered horses, who require a great deal of sustained driving power from their riders. With such, it is more effective to resort to the sitting trot, which gives more power over the horse. It has been observed that the sitting trot presents no problem, even at extended paces, once the horse's back is supple.

Henry Wynmalen *Dressage A Study of the Finer Points of Riding*

The difference in thinking appears to be that, while Seunig is talking of riders who have difficulty remaining seated because of defects in their horses' training, Wynmalen is talking of sitting when a lack of impulsion makes driving necessary, and rising when abundant impulsion makes much driving unnecessary.[2]

However much driving may be necessary, van Schaik makes the point that...

...even when asking for the extended trot, the rider should never lean backwards. It is not only awful to watch...it is also functionally incorrect. It is a misconception...that the rider has to put his weight backwards in order to engage the hindquarters. The rider's centre of gravity behind the plumbline prevents the horse from swinging his hindlegs well forward. At all times the rider has to be with the horse and not behind it.

Dr H.L.M. van Schaik *Misconceptions and Simple Truths in Dressage*

So far as faults in the extended trot are concerned these are, to some extent, a repetition of those seen in the medium gait. Winnett addresses faults in both forms together:

---

[2] When writing this, Wynmalen was presumably not constrained to adhere to FEI competition rules on executing trot work sitting.

The main faults observed in the medium and extended trots are:

1) The hind legs lack engagement and forward thrust, and are often accompanied by a stiff flipping action of the horse's forelegs. This fault can be caused by weak hindquarters, which...can come from lack of gymnastic development or genetic influence. The flipping of the forelegs can be caused by too much tension...

2) The hind legs step wide of the track of the forelegs and the horse transfers weight to his forehand. This fault results from a flaw in conformation; hind legs either set too wide, or bowed...If the hind legs are stepping wide through lack of suppleness or strength, it is probably because the horse is not yet ready for the extended trot.

3) The horse becomes too low in the neck and behind the bit, in which case impulsion will be dissipated and maximum expression of the gait is lost. In the medium and extended trot the poll must remain the highest point, with the head carried slightly in front of the perpendicular to allow the impulsion to flow through the horse's body.

4) Irregular steps. This fault is usually caused by stiffness or weakness in the hindquarters, in which case it is back to the basic lateral exercises in the working trot...

5) Loss of balance. This fault can be caused by any of the foregoing problems...   John Winnett *Dressage as Art in Competition*

While Seunig highlights the following:

Fault: Rushing strides. Frequently a sign that the aids have been given too drastically and too soon and have disturbed the rhythm. *Correction:* Return to the medium trot. Then again very gradually ask for more, after the rhythm has been secured.

Fault: The horse leans on the bit. Despite the pushing of the hind legs, they do not come underneath the horse the way they should and do not flex during the forward movement. The weight is being driven onto the forehand. *Correction:* Frequent transitions between extended and medium trots.

Fault: The hind legs spread…and track to the outside of…the front feet. By this paddling movement, evading to the right and left, they avoid carrying the weight. *Correction:* Through school-ing…lateral bending work.

Fault: The front legs become tense and stretch in a jerky manner. They come down on a point behind that to which the toe is pointed at its highest elevation. *Correction:* The tense strides attest to the fact that there is not enough collection or supple-ness. Symptomatic cure: less rein effect. Lasting cure: submission, suppleness and collection must be improved.

Fault: Horse becomes crooked. *Correction:* At the beginning, a slight natural crookedness may be tolerated so as not to lose the rhythm or enthusiasm…The rhythm and forward movement are more important *for the time being* than the pure straightness. Resistances…which cause this crookedness should be corrected by the appropriate exercises, but never during the extended trot.

Fault: Rider is behind the movement. *Correction:* The upper body should be more vertical.

Waldemar Seunig *The Essence of Horsemanship*

In *Horsemanship,* Seunig makes a point that encompasses sever-al of the above:

If the horse 'falls apart', with neck extended, the accentuated precision of its steps is lost. It will overreach or the traces of its hind legs will grow wider, falling outside the track of the front hoofs instead of reaching beyond them, an indication that there is no longer any harmony between its carriage and its movement.

Waldemar Seunig *Horsemanship*

False movement of the forelegs is widely deprecated:

Extended trot I

The horse's outline should improve and become larger than in the medium trot; the horse should stretch out of himself; the rider should have the feeling of riding uphill, glued to the saddle. The energetic push of the lowered hindquarters encourages the powerful, longer stride. The somewhat heavy neck of the horse could be stretched a little more.

Waldemar Seunig's own drawings of correct (above) and incorrect (right) extended trot from The Essence of Horsemanship.

Another form of faulty trot...is shown by horses that throw the forelegs stiffly from the elbow at the extended trot and hover in the collected trot...a sign of excessive tension of the spinal and related muscles of the trunk.

Ulrik Schramm *The Undisciplined Horse*

Extended trot II

The gait has been increased but along the lines of false tension. The strides are stabbing, with a stiff back, and the neck pulled backward, which should be allowed to stretch more.

Because of the incorrect carriage and the forcing of the trot, it becomes impure, (the left hind foot leaves the ground before the right forefoot, both of which should move simultaneously), that is, the hind is uneven in the sequence.

The stiff, unyielding back does not oscillate, the harmony between the forehand and hindquarters is lost. A horse only using its legs instead of his whole body.

...horses are often forced too soon to extend the trot, gesticulating with the front legs with no thought for the necessary thrusting forward of the hind legs, leading to a concave back.

Nuno Oliveira *Notes and Reminiscences of a Portuguese Rider*

Incorrect extended trot. The horse is on the fore-hand and bearing on the hands. It is badly overbent and its back is rigid. The rider is gripping and jolting the horse's back.

Incorrect extended trot: Ulrik Schramm's own drawing from The Undisciplined Horse.

A horse driven forward by force and held back by the rein might show long strides, but the movement is tense and only the uninitiated gain the impression that the horse is in an advanced stage of training. Richard Wätjen *Dressage Riding*

And Jousseaume advises:

Seek lightness, for, although a little more marked contact...is admissible, nevertheless, the horse must not weight upon the hand; this would prove that the balance has been changed.

André Jousseaume *Progressive Dressage*

Many horses go wide behind and disconnect the trot when the gait is extended. The sole of the hoofs shows. The fault is related to the angulation and construction of the distal end of the tibial and the tibio-tarsal bone of the hock.

Moving wide behind in extended trot. Ulrik Schramm's own drawing and caption from The Undisciplined Horse. *The caption gives a biomechanical reason for the fault, which is additional to those often given by other sources.*

Lengthening the Canter

The biomechanics of medium and extended canter are described by John Winnett:

In the medium canter, the thorax lowers somewhat in its sling, weight is evenly distributed between the haunches and shoulders, the neck lowers and reaches somewhat forward, the poll remains the highest point, and the head is flexed as in collected canter. The horse covers more ground in energetic strides that maintain their three-beat rhythm, the hind legs engaging to a point just behind the line of maximum thrust. The horse remains united, on the bit, and gives the impression that he can return to the collected canter at the slightest suggestion. The medium canter must be ridden just short of the extended canter.

In the extended canter, the thorax lowers completely in its sling and transfers more weight to the horse's forehand, the neck lowers and reaches a fraction more forward than in the medium canter, the head remains flexed at 45 degrees at the poll. The hind legs engage to the line of maximum thrust and the horse covers as much ground as possible in lower, longer and impulsive strides. The horse must give the impression that he is completely...under control, in spite of the greater forward thrust.   John Winnett *Dressage as Art in Competition*

Wynmalen was a great student and advocate of classical dressage, but he always retained an enthusiasm for riding cross-country and was fully at home at the faster gaits. He had a bullish view of extended canter:

The extended canter presents few problems. The horse's range of speed at canter and gallop is almost unlimited and nature puts no difficulties in his way. It is very much easier to obtain a good extended canter than a good extended trot.

Yet the performances seen in the dressage arena are frequently disappointing. Presumably riders become so engrossed in the vastly greater difficulties of the collected exercises, that they overlook the need to keep their horses reasonably trained in the natural extension as well.

Henry Wynmalen *Dressage A Study of the Finer Points of Riding*

While Belasik emphasises the need to accommodate the speed of extended canter, he adds a note of caution which has particular significance for nervous or excitable horses:

The medium and extended canters are both extensions of the canter stride itself. The extended form is the maximum, and the medium is a steady, long stride between the working canter and the extended canter. The canter must obey the same laws of physical motion as all the gaits. As the horse lengthens the stride, it must keep the same tempo. Even when it does, the horse will pick up speed. Unlike racing, speed is not the object of dressage exercises. It is, however, an irrefutable reality. Dressage trainers must learn to take speed into account. For instance, extensions without speed are false.

When a horse is frightened, it will run away from danger. The more frightening the object or situation, the faster it will try to run. Therefore, eliciting speed can induce excitement. This can happen in the extended canter, and the horse has to be trained to handle the excitement of this gait. If tension or fear were to become associated with lengthening the canter, collecting it subtly would be impossible.

Paul Belasik *Dressage for the 21st Century*

Like Wynmalen, Seunig was always prepared to work in the open. Here, he discusses the introduction of medium canter...

As soon as the horse moves off into the canter surely and evenly from the working trot and in the working canter keeps his balance, he can then, in the open and on a straight line, gradually be asked for a medium canter...

The characteristic of the medium canter is a swinging, ground covering series of strides. The horse's outline becomes longer, the contact more definite...However the lively and even rhythm of the strides remains the same. Carriage and submission must not be lost. In spite of the horse being more on the bit, he must not look for support from the hand...The transition between the working and the medium canter should be fluent and unhurried. The drive-on aids must not be abrupt.

...and mentions the interrelationship of the collected and lengthened forms:

Purpose of the medium canter...Increase of impulsion and the accelerating action of the hindquarters, as well as suppleness. The horse is encouraged to use his back more. Preparation for the collected canter, as the medium canter intensifies the spring which will be useful for the shortened gait.

                    Waldemar Seunig   *The Essence of Horsemanship*

Of extended canter he writes:

As in the extended trot, the framework of the horse should be extended by a slight advance of neck and nose, though the timing of the shorter gait is retained. The leaps become flatter and cover more ground, corresponding to the greater driving action exerted by the rider and to the advance of the hands, which are

Medium canter with neck shortened by heavy hands.

Faulty movement in medium canter: Ulrik Schramm's own drawing from The Undisciplined Horse.

in a lower position and afford a more positive contact with the bit as the neck is extended. The rider goes along with the greater speed and extension of the horse's body (without falling forward) in order not to disturb the action by remaining behind.

Waldemar Seunig *Horsemanship*

Adding, in *The Essence of Horsemanship:*

It is derived by gradually increasing demands, when necessary by energetic driving aids...

The long easy canter strides make the horse 'gallop into his neck and onto the bit' throughout the length of the horse's back. Nevertheless, he should always be in the hand of the rider, always be easily controlled...

In discussing the purpose of extended canter, Seunig elaborates on the element of control:

*Purpose:...*Develops propulsion and thrust to their maximum. Serves as a hall-mark for submission, carriage and obedience...A genuinely well-schooled horse should be able even in the extended canter to be ridden with one hand at any time and 'be able to be held with the seat'.

Waldemar Seunig *The Essence of Horsemanship*

While Seunig refers to faults and corrections of the extended canter being the same as for the medium form, Belasik makes the point that:

Paul Belasik riding extended canter, from Belasik's Dressage for the 21st Century.

The most common fault in the extended canter is that the rider does not lengthen the stride in an 'uphill direction' – keeping contact with the reins and guiding the neck up and out so that, as the power increases, the forehand feels as if it climbs. This is possible because lengthening in dressage does not last for too many strides; the acceleration can keep the 'bow of the boat' up if too much weight is not placed there. However, if, in going for maximum reach in the lengthening, the rider drops the reins, allowing the horse's head and neck to drop down, the balance will fall on the forehand...

Paul Belasik *Dressage for the 21st Century*

Richard Wätjen in extended canter, from Wätjen's Dressage Riding.

Smooth, balanced transitions between all gait variants can be seen as proofs of correct training and all are taken seriously by the Masters. However, perhaps because of the power involved, and the sheer speed of the extended gait, the transitions between collected and extended canter invite special comment. Belasik writes:

The extended canter is the largest, longest and consequently the fastest form of canter in dressage. When it is coupled with a transition back to a collected canter, it becomes a very important test of physical and mental agility. The horse must have the physical strength to arrest its considerable mass from its most powerful inertia and smoothly slow it down without changing the tempo of the strides. It must also have the emotional stability to remain obedient to the rider when it is asked to fly powerfully forward for a predetermined distance, and then gather...

The...common area of trouble is in collecting the extended canter when it is done abruptly, or if the horse is not well trained. In such cases, the horse will feel the added work of collecting and deceleration, and change leads to relieve the workload on one hind leg, thus defeating the gymnastic demands of the exercise. The best practice is to gradually develop more strength by working on the transition to and from collection in the medium canter, where it is less taxing and the rider can perfect the fundamentals of the exercise.

Paul Belasik *Dressage for the 21st Century*

Despite his contention that the extended gait, of itself, is relatively easy, Wynmalen approaches the transitions with due care:

The transition from a collected into an extended canter, and vice versa, is not merely a matter of speed. It is a matter also of length of stride and in particular the horse's outward form...During the transition of a collected into an extended canter the horse comes out of the fairly upright form on a comparatively short base into the longer and more horizontal form…

What difficulties there are derive from the transitions. These should be rapid, take no more than a stride or two, yet be free from any semblance of abruptness. They should also be fluent… the horse should appear to flow from one pace and…form into the other without causing a ripple.

Again, it is a matter where horse and rider have to seek for growing mutual understanding…gradually. Riders are rather easily inclined to change their aids too abruptly. Both the increased leg pressure and the longer rein have to take shape together in such a way that the horse is given the necessary time for fluency of execution. As the leg pressure comes on gradually…so the rein lengthens gradually…as the desired extension is achieved, so the leg pressure ceases; the leg comes to rest, remaining just sufficiently vigilant to maintain the horse in the required form.

To succeed in this transition to extension, it is imperative to maintain the horse on the aids all the time; the horse can only be expected to extend fluently if the aids extend fluently with him…

The transition from extension to collection requires equal care; again, any suddenness of execution will surprise the horse…

Henry Wynmalen *Dressage A Study of the Finer Points of Riding*

Finally, Steinbrecht paints a picture of the ideal transition between collected and lengthened canter. His use of the term 'free' for the lengthened form seems very fitting in context. His description of moving the upper body forward to lighten the seat has resonance with the modern, forward position in cross-country canter, usually considered 'post-Caprilli'.

The…ideal collected canter in which each stride gives birth to the next is also the parent of a free canter in which the rider has the uniquely exquisite feeling that he owns the world. Yielding with his hands and moving his upper body…forward relieves the haunches which now let their thrust work with that much more energy and joy. Nevertheless, they are willing, at any moment, when the reins are taken up and the upper body moves back, to take over the load again as desired. It is such an invaluable, precious feeling for the rider to be able to control the motion mechanism with just his hand, or better yet, only the ring finger of his hand; the hind legs require no reminders…because the spirit sets their forces in motion. The weights are distributed as precisely around the rider's seat as they are around the fulcrum of a scale for weighing gold, so that a slight raising or giving of the hand, supported by indiscernible changes in direction of the upper body, is sufficient to put them in motion as desired.

Gustav Steinbrecht *The Gymnasium of the Horse*

Conclusion

In exploring the thoughts of the Masters on collecting and lengthening the horse, we have seen that these forms of movement which, in one sense, might be seen as opposites do, in fact, have much in common. Ultimately, both require great activity of the hindquarters and hind limbs, straightness, suppleness, true 'throughness' of the back and a high level of obedience. These qualities, and the close relationship between collection and extension, are summarised by Hans von Heydebrecht (sometimes rendered von Heydebreck), pupil of Paul Plinzner, commentator upon Steinbrecht and one of the most influential figures of twentieth-century German equitation.

...an imperceptible closing of the rider's fingers must cause the horse to shorten its steps...Conversely, the slightest pressure of the rider's lower legs must produce a determined lengthening of the strides. All the movements must seem totally unconstrained and produced by the rhythmical activity of the muscles of the trunk and spinal column, and the smooth oscillations of the elastic back...Every stride must involve the elastic activity of all the joints of the hindlimbs; according to the degree of collection, the hindlimbs will act more or less as powerful extensible levers to drive the mass forward in long, flowing strides, or as elastic props balancing most of the weight of the body and lightening the forehand. Yet in the extended gaits the hindlimbs must not fail in their balancing role, and in the collected gaits the increased flexion of the hocks must be followed by a powerful thrust. The activity of the muscles of the hindquarters must enable the forefeet to be picked up easily and to alight lightly, the forelimbs to make expansive ground covering gestures, the shoulders to oscillate through a wide arc even in the collected movements, so that the forearms can be lifted to the horizontal and the hooves detached from the ground so easily that they barely seem to touch it before being picked up again.

Hans von Heydebrecht, quoted in Ulrik Schramm's
The Undisciplined Horse

Bibliography

Many of the books cited in this work have been produced in numerous editions, sometimes by more than one publisher. Some, indeed, have been subject to various translations into different languages. Listed below are the editions which have been referred to during the compilation of this book. Where appropriate, information on first publication has been added, to help place the works in historical context.

Albrecht, Kurt, *Principles of Dressage*, J. A. Allen (London) 1993. (1st edn. Verlag ORAC, Vienna 1981).

Belasik, Paul, *Dressage for the 21st Century*, J. A. Allen (London) 2002.

Burger, Üdo, *The Way to Perfect Horsemanship* (tr. Nicole Bartle), J. A. Allen (London) 1998. (First published as *Vollendete Reitkunst*, Paul Parey, Berlin and Hamburg 1959.)

Brooke, Maj.-Gen. Geoffrey, *Horsemanship Dressage & Show-Jumping*, Seeley, Service & Co. Ltd. (London) 1968 (1st edn. 1929).

Cavendish, William, Duke of Newcastle, *A General System of Horsemanship*, facsimile edn. Trafalgar Square Publishing (Vermont) 2000. (First published in France 1658.)

Decarpentry, Gen., *Academic Equitation* (tr. Nicole Bartle), J. A. Allen (London) 1987. (First published in France 1949.)

De la Guérinière, François Robichon, *School of Horsemanship* (tr. Tracy Boucher), J. A. Allen (London) 1994. (First published in a single volume as *Ecole de Cavalerie*, Paris 1733.)

d'Endrödy, Lt. Col. A.L., *Give Your Horse a Chance*, J. A. Allen (London) 1989 (1st edn. 1959.)

Felton, W. Sidney, *Masters of Equitation*, J.A. Allen (London) 1962.

Herbermann, Erik, *Dressage Formula* (3rd edn.), J. A. Allen (London) 1999.

Jousseaume, André, *Progressive Dressage* (tr. Jeanette Vigneron), J. A. Allen (London) 1978. (First published in France by Émile Hazan.)

Knopfhart, Alfred, *Fundamentals of Dressage* (tr. Nicole Bartle), J. A. Allen (London) 1990.

L'Hotte, Gen. Alexis-François, *Questions Équestres* tr. Hilda Nelson in *Alexis-François L'Hotte The Quest For Lightness In Equitation*, J. A. Allen (London) 1997. (*Questions Équestres* first published in France, 1906.)

Müseler, Wilhelm, *Riding Logic* (tr. F.W. Schiller), Eyre Methuen Ltd. (London) 1975. (First published as *Müseler REITLEHRE*, Paul Parey Verlag, Berlin and Hamburg pre.1937.)

Oliveira, Nuno, *Reflections on Equestrian Art* (tr. Phyllis Field), J. A. Allen (London) 1988. (First published as *Reflexions sur l'Art Equestre*, Crépin Leblond, France 1964.)

Notes and Reminiscences of a Portuguese Rider, special publication 1982.

Podhajsky, Alois, *My Horses, My Teachers* (tr. Eva Podhajsky), J. A. Allen (London) 1997. (First published as *Meine Lehrmeister die Pferde*, Nymphenburger Verlagshandlung GmbH., Munich 1968.)

The Complete Training of Horse and Rider (tr. Eva Podhajsky), The Sportsman's Press (London) 1997. (First published as *Die Klassiche Reitkunst*, Nymphenburger Verlagshandlung

GmbH., Munich 1965.)

Schramm, Ulrik, *The Undisciplined Horse* (tr. Nicole Bartle), J. A. Allen (London) 1986. (First published as *Das verrittene Pferd – Ursachen und Weg der Korrektur,* BLV Verlagsgesellschaft, Munich 1983.)

Seunig, Waldemar, *Horsemanship* (tr. Leonard Mins), Robert Hale (London) 1958. (First published in Germany 1941.)

The Essence of Horsemanship (tr. Jacqueline Stirlin Harris), J. A. Allen (London) 1986. (First published in Germany by Erich Hoffmann Verlag 1961.)

Steinbrecht, Gustav, *The Gymnasium of the Horse* (tr. from German 10th edn. Helen K. Buckle), Xenophon Press (Ohio) 1995. (First published in Germany 1885.)

van Schaik, Dr H.L.M., *Misconceptions and Simple Truths in Dressage,* J. A. Allen (London) 1986.

Wätjen, Richard L., *Dressage Riding* (tr. Dr V. Saloschin), J. A. Allen (London) 1973. (First published in Germany 1958.)

Winnett, John, *Dressage as Art in Competition,* J. A. Allen (London) 1993.

Wynmalen, Henry, *Dressage A Study of the Finer Points of Riding,* Wilshire Book Company (California). (First published in 1952.)

Equitation, J. A. Allen (London) 1971. (1st edn.1938.)

Xenophon, The Art of Horsemanship (tr. M.H. Morgan Ph.D), J. A. Allen (London) 1999. (Original Greek text fourth century BC.)

Biographies of Quoted Masters

The following are brief biographies of those whose works are cited in this book. They are given both for reasons of general interest and to assist the reader in placing each author in historical and cultural context.

Albrecht, Kurt Born in Austria in 1920, Albrecht chose a military career and saw active service as an Artillery Commander in the Second World War, before becoming a prisoner of war in Russia. After the war, he joined the Austrian Constabulary and taught equitation at the Constabulary Central School.

Albrecht was a great friend of Hans Handler and, when Handler succeeded Alois Podhajsky as Director of the Spanish Riding School, Albrecht joined the School to assist with administration, being appointed Substitute Director in 1965. In 1974 he succeeded Handler as Director, a post he held until 1985.

From 1973 until 1987 Albrecht was in charge of judges' affairs for the Austrian Equestrian Federation, subsequently playing a leading role in equestrian educational advancement.

Belasik, Paul Born in Buffalo, New York in 1950, Belasik showed a strong affinity with animals from childhood. Early interests included monkey breeding and falconry, as well as horses. This diversity of interest extended beyond the animal kingdom – entering Cornell University as part of the pre-veterinary programme, he graduated with a science degree and had, in the meantime, won prizes for his painting and become a published poet.

By the time of his graduation in 1971, Belasik's career as a horseman had already begun; he taught college courses, evented and competed in dressage at all levels. However, never really excited by competition, he began to focus more on an in-depth study of equitation for its own sake. Initially involved in breeding and training German horses, he focused first upon the German system, broadening and deepening his studies to encompass the different schools of riding. He cites as major influences H.L.M. van Schaik, who instilled in him a love of the classicists and Nuno Oliveira, with whom he spent some time in Portugal. His interest in the philosophical aspects of equitation has been augmented by studies of Zen Buddhism and the martial arts.

Belasik owns and operates a training stable in Pennsylvania, where he works with a broad-based clientele including international competitors, and riders of all levels who have no interest in competition. He also holds clinics and lectures on a national and international basis.

Burger, Üdo (1914–1980) One of Germany's most respected veterinary surgeons and animal psychologists, Burger was an accomplished horseman and a highly respected judge. Involved with horses from an early age, he was reputed to become fretful if unable to spend some time each day in their company. Very obviously a horse lover, he wrote (without giving specific detail) that a horse had actually saved his life in wartime. His professional skills gave him a profound understanding of both the horse's movement and motivation, and he could be blunt in his criticism of rough riding, and of those who made insufficient effort to understand the horse's nature.

Brooke, Maj.-Gen. Geoffrey (1884–1966) Brooke was a genuine all-round horseman. His book *Horsemanship Dressage & Show-Jumping* includes chapters on racing over fences and polo. As a Lt. Colonel he was, in the 1920s, Chief Instructor to the British Cavalry School at Weedon, at a time when British equitation was undergoing a modernising transformation under European influences. A keen student of equitation, he might fairly be described as one of the figures who helped to move British equitation forward.

Cavendish, William, Duke of Newcastle (1593–1676) An English nobleman of great wealth, Cavendish was a cultivated man who wrote plays and poems and became friend and patron to many leading figures in the arts. In 1639 he became a privy counsellor to Charles I and, with the onset of the Civil War, Commander in Chief of the Royalist Northern Army. Initially, he was successful in this role but when the tide of war turned he was obliged to flee to Europe, where he tried in vain to muster support for his king. With Charles I executed and his own estates confiscated, Cavendish settled in exile in Belgium. Here, he devoted his time to training horses and writing *A General System of Horsemanship* – a book which was to have an influence on the thinking of Masters such as de la Guérinière, the Comte d'Aure and Steinbrecht.

With the restoration of the monarchy and the accession of Charles II to the throne in 1660, Cavendish was able to return to England, where the remnants of his estates were returned to him. Although he became a privy counsellor to the new king, he was past the prime of life and had little influence at court. He therefore continued to devote his time to equitation, until failing health obliged him to give up even his own horses. He died in 1676 and was buried at Westminster Abbey.

Decarpentry, General (1878–1956) Born at Lambres, the son and grandson of enthusiastic pupils of François Baucher, Decarpentry soon decided upon a career in the cavalry. Wounded in action at Verdun, he dismissed the permanent damage to his left elbow, saying that it kept his arm bent in the correct position for riding. The injury had no adverse affect on his career, since he was to become commander of cavalry at Saint-Cyr and second in command of the Cadré Noir (1925–31).

From 1939 onward, Decarpentry acted as judge at many international dressage competitions. He also presided over the FEI jury and became President of the FEI Dressage Committee, in which role he was highly influential in developing an international consensus on the aims and judging of competition dressage.

As a rider and equestrian thinker, Decarpentry was by no means confined by the Baucheriste influences of his childhood, as both the references cited in *Academic Equitation*, and his own text shows. It is also evident that he took innovative advantage of the then-young techniques of cinematography to help analyse equine movement.

Decarpentry was a modest man and, although held in great esteem as a rider, he had no desire to participate in competition, his legacy being the skill of his instruction, his work in developing the FEI and the integrity and scholarship which he applied to his equestrian writing.

De la Guérinière, François Robichon (c.1688–1751) Widely regarded as the most influential figure in equestrian history, de la Guérinière was born in Essay, the son of a lawyer. A pupil of

Antoine de Vendeuil, he also had a brother who ran a riding academy in Caen. In 1715, de la Guérinière was granted the title of *écuyer de roi*, and opened a riding academy in Paris, apparently under licence from the Duc d'Anjou.

At his Parisian academy, de la Guérinière taught not only riding, but what was described as 'the complete science of the horse'. By 1730 his reputation was such that he was given the Directorship of the Académie des Tuileries. Despite phenomenal success as a teacher, de la Guérinière was unable to run the academy profitably, and struggled constantly with money – a fact which might endear him to modern-day equestrians.

De la Guérinière's legacy was to develop, from the older style of classical riding, a freedom of movement which characterises modern classical equitation – an achievement which has led him to be described as the 'first of the modern classical riders' (W.S.Felton) and 'undoubtedly the father of modern equitation' (Wynmalen). His lucid work *Ecole de Cavalerie* is quite remarkable for its timeless relevance and wisdom, and continues to be a source of reference for many present-day authorities.

d'Endrödy, Lt. Col. A.L. (1902–1988) A native of Hungary, a country with a great equestrian heritage, d'Endrödy was a member of the Royal Hungarian Olympic three-day event team in 1936, a member of the Hungarian international showjumping team and a champion amateur race rider. The basic idea for *Give Your Horse a Chance* was formulated during the fourteen years which d'Enrödy spent at Orkenytabor, the Hungarian Academy for riding instructors and the training ground for their Olympic team. The book itself was drafted during the three and a half ('sad, lonely') years in which he was prisoner of war in Russian hands, and it may be that the depth of detail in the book is partially attributable to this period of incarceration.

One of d'Endrödy's major influences was as the trainer of Bertalan de Nemethy, coach to the USA Olympic equestrian team in a golden era that produced riders such as William Steinkraus – a great equestrian scholar, who helped refine the translation of *Give Your Horse a Chance* and provided the preface. Largely through his meeting with Col. Frank Weldon at the Stockholm Olympics (where Weldon captained the victorious British Team), d'Endrödy also had a considerable impact on equitation in Britain and spent some time at Badminton, as a guest of the Duke of Beaufort.

Felton, W. Sidney The author of the informative work quoted in the preliminary pages of this book, Felton was born in Massachusetts in 1895. A graduate of Harvard Law School, he served as a US Aviation Officer in the First World War, and subsequently practised law in Boston. A lifelong rider and highly analytical equestrian scholar, he was a keen follower of hounds, an amateur instructor and judge and a leading figure in the organisation of the US Pony Club. Felton was well respected by many leading riders of his era, and the foreword for his *Masters of Equitation* was provided by Henry Wynmalen.

Herbermann, Erik Born in Amsterdam in 1945. Herbermann moved, at an early age with his family to Johannesburg and ten years later, moved to Canada. His initial equestrian training was with Patricia Salt FBHS, herself a pupil of Richard Wätjen and Oberbereiter Lindenbauer at the Spanish Riding School. Herbermann subsequently studied under the celebrated classical riding teacher, Egon von Neindorff.

Now residing in the USA, Herbermann devotes much of his time to lecturing, teaching and conducting clinics internationally. As well as producing three editions of *Dressage Formula*, he has also written numerous articles for equestrian publications.

Herbermann is a staunch advocate of classical ideals, and his ideology is based on an objective study of the horse's nature, which seeks the depth of understanding and quality of work perceived in the greatest of Renaissance Masters. In common with these luminaries, he views equitation as a self-improving art, rooted in the utmost affection and respect for the horse.

Jousseaume, André (d. 1960) A graduate of Saumur and a cavalry officer for most of his lifetime, Jousseaume won the individual silver medal for dressage at the 1932 Olympics when a member of the French gold medal winning team, and repeated this feat in both respects in 1948. He also took the bronze medal in 1952. He retired from the French army with the rank of Colonel and taught at the *Cercle Hippique* until his death.

Knopfhart, Alfred Born in Vienna in 1927, Knopfhart studied economics and business administration, graduating in these subjects in 1951. Having begun riding in Austria at the age of nineteen, he then went to Germany to continue his equestrian studies. In 1962 he became a certified teacher of riding, and was awarded the German silver medal for riders. Since that time, he has worked continually as a trainer of horses and riders at all levels up to Grand Prix and, since 1989, has given annual clinics at several dressage centres in the USA.

In 1964, Knopfhart became a certified judge for dressage, showjumping and eventing; in 1968 an official of the Austrian Horse Show Association and in 1970 an international FEI dressage judge. From 1986–96, he headed the official body of Austrian show judges.

In addition to lecturing at the University of Veterinary Medicine, Vienna, Knopfhart has written three books and many articles on equestrian issues.

L'Hotte, Gen. Alexis-François (1825–1904) A son and grandson of French cavalrymen, L'Hotte was, from an early age, a keen student of the equestrian writings of the old French Masters – much to the detriment of his academic education. He initially attended the military academy of Saint-Cyr as a young cadet, being sent on to pursue his equestrian interests at Saumur, since the cavalry section at Saint-Cyr had been closed. Despite some youthful indiscipline, he eventually attained the rank of General, and became Commandant of the re-opened cavalry section at Saint-Cyr, and subsequently of Saumur.

It is of great interest to students of equestrian history that L'Hotte was a pupil of both François Baucher and Comte D'Aure, two highly influential figures who not only practised different styles of equitation, but were considered rivals and had their own factions of supporters. L'Hotte was a great note-taker, and his anecdotes about and comparisons of these two figures make fascinating reading.

L'Hotte himself was considered to be one of the most outstanding *écuyers* of a golden age: he originated the phrase 'equestrian tact' and the famous maxim 'calm, forward and straight.'

Müseler, Wilhelm (1887–1952) Born in Berlin, Müseler was, in his youth, a fine athlete – he held the German record for the 100m sprint. Following a grammar school education, he embarked upon a career as a cavalry officer. During the years preceding the First World War, he competed with great success at dressage and showjumping, and was a member of the German Olympic equestrian team. However, upon being told by his commanding officer that he should make his career 'with his intellect rather than his backside', he intensified his commitment to his primary role as an officer. His military abilities are evidenced by the fact that, by 1918, he had become the youngest Major on the General Staff. Later in life, when recalled to the General Staff at the onset of World War II, he was to attain the rank of General.

Leaving the army after the end of the First World War, Müseler again committed himself to equitation, becoming Director of Tattersall Beermann, then the largest equestrian centre in Berlin. In this role, his emphasis shifted away from active competition and towards training horses and riders and organising equestrian events. He also became Master of the Berlin Hunting Society and President of the German Association of Hunting Clubs.

In 1931, health problems compelled him to cease his riding activities. *Riding Logic,* written by way of a conclusion, was originally intended for the academic equestrian societies he had founded. Once published, however, the book became a bestseller, appearing in many editions and many languages. From 1932 onward, Müseler also wrote books on the history of art, one of which sold over a million copies – he considered these books the most important work of his life.

Oliveira, Nuno (d.1989) This great Portuguese Master began his career as a pupil of Joaquin Gonzales de Miranda, former Master of the Horse to the Portuguese Royal Family. After Miranda's death, Oliveira trained horses first for cavalry officers and a dealer, then for one of Miranda's pupils, Senōr Chefalenez. Subsequently, a friend and student, Manual de Barros asked him to train at his brother-in-law's stud where, in addition to having many good horses to ride, he also had at his disposal a large equestrian library. During this period, he met Alois Podhajsky when they both rode at an exhibition in the Campo Grande and the pair became firm friends.

During the 1950s, Oliveira attracted a number of highly talented pupils, and opened his riding school at Quinta do Chafaris. He also began to write articles (and subsequently, books) on equitation, while a pupil organised a weekly TV programme showing his lessons.

In 1961 he gave his first exhibition abroad, in Switzerland, and the following year he rode in the Winter Circus in Paris, where he met and established a lasting relationship with Capt. Durand, later to be Commander of the Cadre Noir.

Subsequent years saw a further influx of pupils, many from abroad, and numerous clinics and exhibitions throughout Europe, North and South America and Australia, which continued up to the time of his death.

Podhajsky, Alois (1899–1973) The son of an Austro-Hungarian cavalry officer, Podhajsky joined a dragoon regiment aged seventeen and received regular lessons from Capt. Count Telekei, whom he described as an excellent instructor.

Although in a cavalry regiment, Podhajsky spent much of the First World War on foot. After the war, following the demise of the Austro-Hungarian Empire, he was admitted to the new Federal Army, and riding once again became part of his career. Having achieved considerable success in showjumping, he was encouraged by his colonel to study dressage, which he found further improved his horse's jumping. Transferred to advanced training at the cavalry school at Schlosshof, he began to achieve international success in dressage, showjumping and three-day events.

In 1933, he was sent to the Spanish Riding School, where he studied under luminaries such as Polak, Zrust and Lindenbauer. Their influence helped him to train his own horses to Grand

Prix level and to win a bronze medal for dressage at the 1936 Olympics.

From 1934–8 he worked as a cavalry instructor, first in Austria and then in Germany. In 1938 Austria was annexed by Germany, and the Spanish Riding School was placed under the command of the German Army. When, in 1939, Podhajsky became Director of the Spanish Riding School, he managed to convince senior German officers, who were experienced horsemen, of the value of the School. By this, and other actions in that period, Podhajsky was instrumental in protecting the School for posterity.

In the post-war years, Podhajsky competed abroad both with his own horses and the School's Lipizzaners. He also took the Spanish Riding School on a number of foreign tours, including a major tour of the USA shortly before his retirement in 1964.

Schramm, Ulrik (1912–1995) A vastly experienced German horseman and equestrian author, who was dedicated to the proper education of horses for all disciplines. His philosophy is expounded in his own words: 'Seat is obviously an essential element in mastery of the horse, but the rider's head is surely as important as his seat'; 'Riding is not truly a sport if unity of mind does not exist between rider and horse'. A talented artist, Schramm used his own mild caricatures of horses and riders to emphasise the points made in his writing.

Seunig, Waldemar (1887–1976) Born in the then Duchy of Krain, Seunig was educated at a military academy in Austria and entered the cavalry. He subsequently attended the Riding Instructors' Institute in Vienna, where he became a pupil of the famous Josipovich. Then, in the political upheaval of the times, he was more or less repatriated (to what was by that time Slovenia, in Yugoslavia).

Since, by then, he had established a considerable reputation, he was offered the post of Master of the Horse at the Yugoslavian Royal Court. This he accepted, on condition that he first spent a year at the French Cavalry School at Saumur, and six months at the Royal Mews in London (to learn protocol). Subsequently, he was also granted a year at the Spanish Riding School, back in Vienna.

Following a decline of royal interest in riding, Seunig became Chief Riding Master of the Yugoslavian Cavalry School in 1930. However, when offered promotion to General, he retired instead, since this would have entailed active service for a country for which he had no patriotic feelings.

After this retirement he kept riding, and, an Olympic competitor himself, also coached the German team that was successful in the Berlin Olympics. When, during the Second World War, Slovenian partisans destroyed his home, he moved to Germany where he gained high office as an equestrian instructor in the army.

After the war, he travelled extensively and became renowned as a rider, teacher and international judge. A great lover of literature, Seunig was also a keen artist and many of his own drawings adorn his books.

Steinbrecht, Gustav (1808–1885) Born in Saxony, Steinbrecht studied veterinary medicine before becoming a pupil of Louis Seeger, one of the most influential trainers of the nineteent century, who had, himself, been a pupil of Weyrother, a celebrated figure of the Spanish Riding School.

Steinbrecht stayed with Seeger for eight years, during which time he married Seeger's niece and became an accomplished *écuyer*. He then took over direction of a manège in Magdeburg, where he remained for a further eight years, before rejoining Seeger.

In 1849, Steinbrecht became director of Seeger's establishment and, at about this time, began to make the notes that were to form the basis of *The Gymnasium of the Horse*. Seeger himself disagreed with the teachings of François Baucher – also active at this time – preferring methods and principles expounded by de la Guérinière. That Steinbrecht shared Seeger's view of Baucher is obvious from the vigorous attacks upon Baucher's method which permeate *The Gymnasium of the Horse*.

As Steinbrecht's health failed, he entrusted the completion of his book to his pupil/disciple, Paul Plinzner. Through Plinzner, and Plinzner's eminent pupil, Hans von Heydebreck, the work of Steinbrecht had a major influence on the formulation of the German [army] Riding Rules, and on German equitation in general.

van Schaik, Dr H.L.M. (1899–1991) Born in Holland, Dr van Schaik began his riding career as a showjumper. In this discipline, he represented his country many times with conspicuous success: in 1936 he was a member of the team that won silver at the Berlin Olympics. Gradually, however, his interest turned more and more towards dressage.

After the war, he settled in the USA, where he opened a riding academy and became highly respected as a rider, trainer and judge. Throughout the 1960s, 70s and 80s, he was one of a number of riders from the classical mould who were increasingly concerned that competition dressage was departing from classical principles. His book *Misconceptions and Simple Truths in Dressage* has its roots in articles he wrote to try to reverse that trend.

Wätjen, Richard L. (b. 1891) Early backing from his parents enabled Richard Wätjen to embark upon a career devoted entirely to equitation – and he did not squander this privileged position. After studying at Trakehen and Graditz, both German government studs, he spent six years (1916–21) as a pupil of the Spanish Riding School, then stayed on for a further six years as a guest amateur instructor and trainer.

In 1925, he moved to Berlin and began training horses and riders on a professional basis. This scheme proved highly successful: his pupils achieved great national and international success, and he was instrumental in training several Olympic teams, including the British team which competed at Helsinki in 1952.

As a rider, he produced many horses of various breeds to the highest standards, and achieved international success competing in both dressage and showjumping, two of his best-known horses being Burgsdorff and Wotan. Many authorities regard him as being one of the most elegant riders of his era.

Winnett, John Born in Los Angeles in 1928, Winnett was educated in Paris, where he was introduced to riding in the French classical tradition by Victor Laurent, a retired officer from Saumur who had studied under the doctrine of L'Hotte. Winnett subsequently became interested in showjumping and was instructed according to the methods of Col. Danloux, who had refined principles introduced by Federico Caprilli. He became French Junior National Champion in 1945.

As an adult Winnett 'abandoned serious riding to pursue a career' in the Indian sub-continent, Europe and subsequently New York. This 'abandonment' did not prevent him from amateur race-riding, playing polo and, indeed, representing the USA in the 1952 World Showjumping Championships.

Retiring early from a successful career, Winnett turned his full concentration upon horses and went to Germany, to study with Reiner Klimke. In Germany, he was initially surprised to discover a very free-moving style of equitation which traced back to the teachings of de la Guérinière. Much influenced by these German methods, to which he added a detailed study of equine biomechanics, Winnett achieved great success in competition dressage, becoming riding captain of the American team at the 1972 Olympics and continuing to represent his country at the highest levels throughout the 1970s and 1980s.

Wynmalen, Henry (1889–1964) Undoubtedly one of the most influential figures in British equitation, Wynmalen was Dutch by birth and spent his early life in Holland, coming to England in 1927. An engineer by profession, Wynmalen's many interests included yachting, motor rallying and aviation. A flying accident, which left a legacy of back trouble, resulted in Wynmalen adopting a somewhat individualistic riding posture, but did not prevent him from being a consummate all-round horseman.

His early years were devoted primarily to showjumping, cross-country riding and racing, and he was, for many years, MFH to the Woodland Hunt. Always concerned with the correct schooling of horses, and renowned for his quiet, patient methods, he became increasingly interested in classical dressage. In 1948, he won the British Dressage Championship, and followed this with many other successes. His displays at the Royal Windsor Show, and the ease with which his 'dressage' horses performed across country, served to ignite a greater interest in dressage in Britain – an interest he helped to promote with no reduction in his enthusiasm for the other disciplines.

A highly successful breeder and exhibitor of show horses, a respected judge and President of the Arab Horse Society,

Wynmalen also served on the Executive Council of the BHS. Largely responsible for organising the horse trials competition at the 1948 (London) Olympics, he played a major role in instigating one-day events and, for some years, served as President of the Jury at Badminton horse trials.

Xenophon (430–354BC) A Greek historian, philosopher and military commander, Xenophon wrote one of the earliest books on riding, which is now known as *The Art of Horsemanship*. While his book would not, nowadays, be considered of particular value in terms of its technical content, it is nevertheless true that Xenophon had a sound grasp of many of the principles of equitation. What is more remarkable about his work is his humane understanding of equine psychology, which may not have been equalled anywhere until well into the Renaissance era. It is chiefly this characteristic, so far in advance of his time, that has earned the respect of many eminent equestrians.